The
Culture
We
Deserve

Also by Jacques Barzun

Begin Here

Berlioz and the Romantic Century

Classic, Romantic, and Modern

Clio and the Doctors

Critical Questions

Darwin, Marx, Wagner

The Energies of Art

From Dawn to Decadence

The House of Intellect

Simple and Direct

A Stroll With William James

Use and Abuse of Art

The Culture We Deserve

Jacques Barzun

Arthur Krystal, Editor

Wesleyan University Press
Middletown, Connecticut

Published by Wesleyan University Press,
Middletown, CT 06459
www.wesleyan.edu/wespress

Printed in the United States of America   10 9 8

ISBN: 978-0-8195-6237-1

Library of Congress Cataloging-in-Publication Data
Barzun, Jacques, 1907–
      The culture we deserve.
      Includes index.
         1. Learning and scholarship. 2. Humanities.
      3. Civilization, Modern—20th century—Philosophy.
      I. Krystal, Arthur. II. Title.
      AZ221.B29   1989   001.2   88-33927

Contents

Author's Note

When at the instance of the publisher I agreed to put together some essays written in the eighties on the theme of contemporary culture, I was fortunate enough to find a helping hand in the person of Arthur Krystal, whose experience as a critic and editor lightened for me the task of preparing the typescript and seeing it through the press. In addition, Jeannette Hopkins, the instigator of the project at Wesleyan, gave the text careful reading and collating. Following their indications, I removed topical allusions, unwanted repetitions, verbal ambiguities, and traces of platform rhetoric. I am deeply grateful to both these friends for sparing me chores and for suggesting judicious improvements.

But I alone am responsible for the arrangement that keeps essays ostensibly on the same topic at a distance from each other, instead of in immediate sequence. The aim of separation is to bring out the less visible connections that cut across the obvious ones. Thus the first three chapters deal with current ways of handling the products of culture; the next four testify to society's consciousness of itself; the next two criticize the attitudes taught in colleges about the liberal and the fine arts; and the last three consider the plausible signs that civilization is in decline.

The essence of culture is interpenetration. From any part of it the searching eye will discover connections with another part seemingly remote. If from my descriptions the reader finds this wide-angled view sharpened or expanded, my purpose in publishing these pages will have been served.

About forty years ago certain persons went up to Laputa, either upon business or diversion, and upon their return began to dislike the management of everything below, and fell into schemes of putting all arts, sciences, languages, and mechanics upon a new foot. To this end they procured a royal patent for erecting an Academy of Projectors in Lagado. Every room hath in it one or more projectors. The first man I saw had been eight years extracting sunbeams out of cucumbers.

—Swift: *Gulliver's Travels*, Part III, chs. 4–5

Why did the old Folly end now, and no later? Why did the modern Wisdom begin now, and no sooner? What were we the worse for the former Folly, what the better for the succeeding Wisdom?

—Rabelais, Prologue to Book V

Decadence was brought about by doing work too easily and being too lazy to do it well, by a surfeit of fine art and a love of the bizarre.

—Voltaire: *The Princess of Babylon*

The Culture We Deserve

Culture High and Dry

By now the word *culture* has been used with so many different meanings that its use creates in the alert reader a degree of confusion. The anthropologists started the trouble by using *culture* to mean all the modes of belief and behavior of a tribe or people. The word *society* was available, but it looked as if pre-empted by the sociologists; the younger science wanted a word of its own. From the anthropologists the public picked up the word *culture* in its overarching meaning, and then proceeded to reapply it for various purposes. For example, the artist is "conditioned by his culture" (meaning social circumstances); he also fights against his culture (meaning certain beliefs and mores). Again, culture (meaning social restraints) makes neurotics—they are the ones who can't fight back. Not long after such twists and turns the term *culture* began to split like the atom, and we have had to cope with the two cultures, the counterculture, ethnic culture, and any number of subcultures. Culture now is any chunk of social reality you like or dislike.

In the present discussion I mean by culture the traditional things of the mind and spirit, the interests and abilities acquired by taking thought; in short, the effort that used to be called cultivation—cultivation of the self. This original meaning, as used, say, by Matthew Arnold in *Culture and Anarchy*, is obviously a metaphor. It is based on *agri*culture—the tilling of the soil, planting of seeds, and reaping a harvest of nourishing things. We still acknowledge that meaning when we use the phrases "a man or woman of culture," "a cultivated person." The implication is that the raw substance of the

3

creature has been turned over, plowed, and seeded with good germs, and in such a way that the potentialities of both the human being and what has been implanted are visibly and usefully realized.

Since *culture* is no longer clear, why not simply say "the educated man or woman"? The answer is that the word *educate* has been just as badly tossed about as the other. No need to give a parallel account of its tribulations. Today anybody with a diploma from any institution calling itself educational is counted among the educated, while the disparate doings of our elementary and high schools are also called education. The difference between *instruction* and *education* has been forgotten, and it is usual, commonplace, to hear people say that in this or that school or college, students are *given* an education.

My concern, then, is with something other than *culture* and *education* as these terms are bandied about. Culture and education are qualities found in persons who have first been taught to read and write and then have managed, against heavy odds, to cultivate their minds, to educate themselves. In every generation persons are born with the desire for this kind of exercise, just as others are born with the desire to exercise their bodies and become athletes. But it is also true that many others, if encouraged, can develop these same desires and become, in their measure, athletic or cultivated or both.

If for any reason we are curious about this component of civilization—of present or past civilizations—we try to guess at the number of such people compared with the size of the population, and we look into the institutions that serve the various interests called cultural. For it is evident that when the contents of culture have been garnered over many centuries, no individual—indeed, no generation of individuals—can possess the whole heritage, much less transmit it without loss or distortion. Special guardians and repositories are needed; hence libraries, museums, opera houses, and other groupings for the accumulation of cultural works, the continuity of cultural enjoyment, the facilitation of cultural production.

As the years pass, there is more and more cultural stuff to house, classify, docket, consult, and teach—let alone discover, remember, and enjoy. Today in the Western world we stand on top of half a millennium of unbroken cultural creation and preservation, and we keep adding large amounts of kindred material from other civilizations, plus the steady accretion of rare discoveries from the remote past: we now have a hymn from the Babylonians, ancient Egyptian love lyrics, paintings from Cro-Magnon caves. No doubt exploration under the sea will shortly tell us the words of the song that the sirens sang to Ulysses.

Anybody would say that outwardly we handle this growing treasure with great efficiency and profound respect. The nineteenth century established both the cult of art and the passion for history. So we collect everything and, in the professional jargon, "make it available." Nor is our concern with culture all retrospect and antiquarianism. We believe in encouraging the modern and the young. Amateur music, painting, theatricals, poetry readings, and writing workshops thrive all over the land, thanks not only to natural desire but also to private and public money. It would seem that this century of wars and massacres and failing powers of governance is redeemed by a high degree of true culture.

Yet I venture to think that in the qualitative, honorific sense, culture—cultivation—is declining. It is doing so virtually in proportion as the various cultural endeavors—all this collecting and exhibiting and performing and encouraging—grow and spread with well-meant public and private support. The reason is not merely that the very abundance tends to distract attention, to leave no time for digesting and meditating upon the experience, though that is an important drawback of the glut. There is a deeper reason, which can be put in one word: *self-consciousness.*

To begin with, modern society is concerned and vocal about art-and-culture—it is one word, and it means prestige and money. The New York State Senate has a Special Committee on the Culture Industry, which is doubtless not unique. Private and public funds ebb and flow in and out of that corner of the economy, and there is among artists and art lovers a permanent indignation about the neglect of their special-interest group. Self-consciousness is manifest. We go at the arts with deliberate intent to commit an aesthetic act, and at our heels is a census taker. If a visitor from outer space were to ask any well-informed American, on a campus or at some artistic gathering, Tell me how I can find the best evidences of high culture in this country, the answer would very likely be, Go to our colleges and universities—but, of course, take a look at our many great museums, libraries, and concert societies, and read our literary quarterlies. I am fairly sure that universities would be mentioned first, and I am certain that the informant would list *institutions*, not individuals or well-known circles—self-selected groups of people.

The unspoken assumption would be that in these academic and other establishments the persons in charge are cultivated men and women, capable of representing to a stranger the state of Western culture today. That sounds plausible, yet I think the visitor from afar would be repeatedly disappointed in his search. He would find extraordinarily bright people, often very learned people, dedicated to the *idea* of a particular art, to its scholarship or performing or critical theory, and gifted moreover with practical competence in managing things, but too busy handling their cultural assignment to cultivate themselves within it or beyond it. If some topic outside that chosen field came up in conversation, the modest disclaimer would be, Oh, as to that, you'll have to see Jones, the musicologist (or Robinson, the curator of prints and engravings; or Smith, our theater man).

I am not simply restating the well-known fact of specialism. What I am pointing to is something implicit in specialism but rarely noticed or expressed, namely, that through specialism culture is *delegated* to the experts; it is no longer the property of whoever wants to partake of it for the good of his soul. One obvious consequence is the fragmentation that everybody deplores and nobody does anything about. The expert takes a little subject for his province—and remains a provincial all his life. But there is worse. By this delegation of culture the importance of art and the humanities is shifted to a new ground. These good things are no longer valuable for their direct effect on the head-and-heart; they become valuable as professions, as means of livelihood, as badges of honor, as goods to be marketed, as components of the culture industry.

Some may think that I have misstated part of the situation. It is still true that anyone may partake; in fact, the path is made easy and smooth for the amateur in a dozen ways. But under the influence of that very help from the guardians and from their inspiring example, the amateur rapidly becomes another expert, another delegate. The collector of paintings is a mine of information about his collection; the chamber-music player can talk at length about the string-quartet literature; the devotee of Jane Austen is soon recognizable as a reader of novels who has barely heard of Dickens—and so on for ballet, film, sculpture, and architecture; or crosswise, for the ancient, medieval, and other centuries, styles, or schools. The interest displayed is scarcely cultural; it is not for self-cultivation; rather, it is, in sociological idiom, a leisure-time activity, like being a baseball fan. Both hobbies generate the same pedantic, miserlike heaping up of factual knowledge. One illustration tells the tale: there are said to be more than three hundred societies devoted each to a single author, the membership being made up almost entirely of amateurs who do research, meet and confer on points of scholarship, and—inevitably—publish a newsletter.

It may be asked why I call this modern way of handling the stuff of culture a regrettable sign of self-consciousness. Some may say, the arts, lacking patronage, have found shelter in the university; the cognate institutions have grown more and more professional so as to serve knowledgeable audiences; the government and foundations have set up the project-and-grant system in answer to public demand; the many connoisseurs have innocently fallen into line. All this has taken place gradually, without foresight or warning as to consequences. Indeed, many people, unaware of anything having changed, think it all natural. What is fully conscious about the whole is the fierce resolve behind the effort, the programs with their rules and definitions, the departments with their subspecialties—a nineteenth-century man, a Renaissance woman, a Milton scholar who justifies the poet's ways in class Monday, Wednesday, and Friday at ten. Out of this benevolent regimentation, coupled with the elective system, comes the principle that everybody must at some time—usually in college—get a dose of this well-organized pharmacopoeia.

How this scheme affects the public is shown vividly in the advertiser's portrait of That Cosmopolitan Girl. She talks about herself, and her remarks let us see into an important part of the public mind. Here is one of her characteristic meditations:

Can a girl be *too* busy? I'm taking seventeen units at Princeton, pushing on with my career during vacations and school breaks, study singing and dancing when I can, try never to lose track of my five closest chums, steal the time for Michael Jackson *and* Thomas Hardy, work for an antidrug program for kids and, oh yes, I hang out with three horses, three cats, two birds and my dog Jack. My favorite magazine says "too busy" just means you don't want to miss anything. . . . I love that magazine. I guess you could say I'm That COSMOPOLITAN Girl.

After college, in her middle life, Michael Jackson may well recede and Thomas Hardy gain the upper hand, directing her into the kind of connoisseurship I have described. In one sense, scholarship, the university, will have won another recruit. Or the college exposure may fail, the seventeen units adding up to zero.

But is not a life of culture possible outside the actual and figurative walls of the academy? Hardly any. The public mind is assailed from all sides by the products of scholarly thought. At exhibitions of paintings and sculptures, explanations and judgments are given from tapes through earphones or posted in print next to each work. At concerts the listener begins by reading program notes. All but the newest books come supplied with introductions and notes. Reference books are as numerous as real books—manuals, digests, and dictionaries on every subject, which deliver information in capsule form.

Nor is this dry diet the only deprivation. It used to be that unassuming readers cultivated their minds through history which feeds curiosity and furnishes the imagination. Good histories, moreover, are part of literature. Today that source of culture has dried up too: it has been delegated, and professional historians no longer write for the public but for one another. And latterly their narrow subjects have ceased to be historical and become sociological or psychiatric, rarely narrative. Such topics are not expected to attract the general reader. He or she very likely falls back on biography, which remains a popular genre. But when the work is not also a piece of retrospective psychiatry, it is often an undigested mass of detail, mostly gossip gathered from interviews with surviving friends and enemies of the deceased.

Another cultural exercise of mind formerly open to the unacademic was philosophy. The great questions about being and becoming, knowledge and sense impressions, the test of truth, and the contradictions of common sense have not lost their fascination, but philosophers no longer write for the intelligent, only for their fellow professionals. The few thousand academic philosophers in the world do not stint themselves: they maintain more than seventy learned journals. But in the handful that cover more than one subdivision of philosophy, any given philosopher can hardly follow more than one or two articles in each issue. This hermetic condition is attributed to "technical problems" in the subject. Since William James, Russell, and Whitehead, philosophy, like history, has been confiscated by scholarship and locked away from the contamination of cultural use.

I have no wish to reprove any honest use of the intellect. My aim is only to contrast implicit claims with actual results, profession with performance; and to ascribe discrepancy not to individual fault but to the temper of the world and the deceitful march of time. We are mistaken when we believe that culture and the humanities are being served by scholarship. The truth is that art and culture do not belong in a university. It cannot be a home for them, because culture proper and scholarship proper are diametrically opposed. Think back to the antecedents of scholarship as we know it. Its origins lie in the desire, at the time of the Renaissance, to establish clear and correct versions of the ancient classics. Scholarship remained a textual, linguistic enterprise through much of the last century, as we are reminded by Nietzsche's use of the phrase *Wir Philologen*—"we philologists," meaning "we scholars"—as a chapter title in 1885.

The methods and conventions of textual critics spread beyond their first domain and into other subjects, notably historiography, and from there it was a natural step to adapt these ways to the physical and the social sciences. When these became popularized, scholarly habits became general; nowadays one comes across needlessly exact references in weekly magazines, and bibliographies and other scholarly apparatus in business and government documents.

In all these, the original intention of scholarship persists, whether duly or poorly carried out: it is *analysis*; that is, the narrow scrutiny of an object for the purpose of drawing conclusions. These in turn must be supported by arguments and must take into account the previous arguments of others, known as "the literature" of the subject. It is clear that as the analysts multiply and the literature accumulates, the subject that anyone is able to deal with grows smaller. In other words, specialization is unavoidable; and thus it is that specialism, which is a state of mind, follows specialization, which is a practical necessity.

If at any time in this development thoughtful people had doubts about the desirability of subjecting the fruits of culture to scholarship—to specialism—those doubts were overridden by the success of the natural sciences. There the subject matter seemed not merely to call for specializing but also to lend itself to endless subdivision. The bits and pieces were easily reunited by mathematics, by accepted principles universally applicable, and by the permanent one-ness of nature itself. Thus the by-product of the great achievement of science is that everybody's mind is now shaped from the cradle to desire and to trust analysis exclusively. The best minds are analytic engines, ready to work on any material.

What is analysis? It is what the word means in Greek: to break down. Specialization and analysis go together; they are the same process at different levels of any subject—you break up the whole domain, then you break down the smaller portions ad infinitum. The purpose of analysis is to show what little things big things are made of and how the little bits fit together to produce the whole. The only difficulty is to decide what the bits are and when one has got hold of every separate kind. Right now nuclear physicists seem to be finding bits in an endless series.

But the same human mind that has created science by the analytical method can work in an entirely different way. The mathematician-philosopher Pascal pointed this out 350 years ago. He called the way of analysis the "geometrical bent." It deals with simple things like angles or straight lines or atoms or molecular pressure. They are simple because they are well defined, not because they are familiar. Most of them are not; some of them are not even visible or tangible. But being well defined, they do not change when they are talked about and can thus be represented by numbers. The principles of mathematics and a few others then supply the rules for dealing with the permutations of these clear and simple unchangeables.

The other use, direction, or bent, Pascal called the *esprit de finesse*—we might call it "intuitive understanding." It goes about its business just the other way. It does not analyze, does not break things down into parts, but seizes upon the character of the whole altogether, by inspection. Since in this kind of survey there are no definable parts, there is nothing to count and there are no fixed principles to apply. The understanding derived from the experience is direct, and because it lacks definitions, principles, and numbers, this understanding is not readily conveyed to somebody else; it can only be suggested in words that offer analogies—by imagery. Hence no universal agreement is possible on these objects and their significance.

Now, the things that make up culture are understood and remembered and enjoyed by mental finesse; they are for inspection as wholes, not for analysis and measurement; they lack definable, unchangeable parts.

One may say, "But that's contrary to fact! Poets and composers themselves divide their works into parts. Goethe's *Faust* has Part I and Part II; Beethoven's symphonies have not only four parts but shorter ones within each movement; and at any time within these there are upper parts and bass, eight vocal parts in the last movement of the Ninth Symphony, and so on. Likewise with painting and sculpture: we can all see or find parts." All this is true, but only in a metaphorical sense. Actually, the parts have no independent existence. Part I of *Faust* requires Part II for its full understanding—and a critic has no sooner said that than another critic says, "Nonsense! Part I can stand alone. Part II is a farrago of inferior episodes that destroy the effect of the real masterpiece"; and he proves it by quotations and arguments. The first critic proved his point too, and here we are, bystanders in the midst of the critical chaos, where nearly every critic and scholar proves his case and no two cases are—on all fours.

The last example is a very primitive instance of the dissensus about a work of art. The elaborations of modern scholarship go far beyond assertion and counterassertion on such simple matters of merit and quality. Literary scholarship still clings to the text, but, believing in analysis, subjects it to a variety of so-called methods. There is source-hunting to detect influence and show how the great work was put together like a jigsaw puzzle; there is theme analysis to find out what the work is *really* about; there is the search for myth and symbol to dig out the hidden meanings of the words; there is the Marxist or other sociological method to prove how evil capitalism or Victorianism or male domination or life itself can be; there is the psychoanalytic method to discover what drove the poor puppet of an artist to write or compose as he did. Not long ago, a musically equipped psychoanalyst produced an interpretation of Bach's thirty "Goldberg Variations." One hopes he will also interpret Count Keyserling, for the count commissioned the variations and had Goldberg play them to him every night to lull him to sleep.

In the study of literature these analytic methods are supplemented by critical theory, since art as a whole and all its genres are supposed to follow theory the way an engine's performance answers to thermodynamics. There are theories of comedy and of tragedy, of satire and of lyric poetry, in addition to which there are theories of criticism: new criticism, which applies close reading to ascertain whether the metaphors "work out"; structural criticism, which tests for solidity of parts and their attachments; deconstructivism, which seems to teach that the real author is the language he uses and the real work is the reader in his armchair.

It is not surprising that the flowering of methods has taken place in the university, for that institution has the duty to teach. And any subject, to be teachable, must be presented in systematic form. There must be definitions, principles, methods for covering and mastering the ground. I have used literature as illustrative, because its academic treatment is the most familiar, but there are corresponding methods in other departments. Art history devotes itself to iconography—translating symbols in a painting or finding sources and parallels in other paintings or in literature. Musicology analyzes styles, classifies technical devices, or tests accomplishment by one or another method, such as Schenker analysis. A distinguished analyzer has been heard to say that the flaw in the first movement of Beethoven's "Eroica" Symphony was easily remediable, which would have made it perfect. When an astonished amateur asked, "If Beethoven had telephoned you about the place you object to, you could have told him what to do?" he replied, "Yes, indeed."

The magic spell of science is evident in these various procedures: scholarship has yielded to the irresistible pull that science exerts on our minds by its self-confidence and the promise of certified knowledge. But, to repeat, the objects of culture are not analyzable, not graspable by the geometrical mind. Great works of art are great by virture of being syntheses of the world; they qualify as art by fusing form and contents into an indivisible whole; what they offer is not "discourse about," nor a cipher to be decoded, but a prolonged incitement to finesse. So it is paradoxical that our way of introducing young minds to such works should be the way of scholarship.

There is no use asking how earlier generations reconciled college and university teaching with the demands of genuine culture, for the idea of *studying* literature, *studying* past art is extremely recent. Down to the 1850s there were no courses in those subjects; they were not *subjects* at all. And even after they came in, as a hoped-for antidote to science and political economy, nobody believed that contemporary art and literature should be or could be studied. It was felt, quite rightly, that it is extremely difficult to tell which contemporary artists are worth close attention, and it was believed that, good or bad, those artists would be read or followed by the public for pleasure and edification, not for points credit. Indeed, it was expected that the great innovative artist would appeal directly to the young, who would read him in secret, or go to hear his music, or see his paintings in some out-of-the-way place, and thus undergo at first hand, without pedagogy, the formative impress of the latest phase of culture.

As things stand now, the new is brought on campus and dissected before the body has had time to cool. The young doubtless enjoy the "relevance" of "up-to-date" novelties, but that pleasure is dimmed by the required application of methods. As for the sense of continuity or contrast with earlier models and masterpieces, it is compromised by the double interference of remoteness in time and the uniform brunt of analysis. To be sure, exceptions occur wherever the guide is a cultured mind. But it is fair to say that the modern student, the "major" in English or American studies or in one of the other departments, has no cultivating encounter with the works of art he or she has been assigned. George Eliot has been read for the plight of women or for images of running water; the Post-Impressionists testify to sordid society and individual alienation; the rise and fall of the sonata form demonstrates that no music should have been written after 1830.

In the graduate school we see the final turn given to the conversion of culture into industry. "Publish or perish" ensures that every scrap of cultural raw material shall be manufactured into a product for prestige or promotion, the sign of success being the treatment of some original topic according to an accepted method. In search of "findings" and talking like physicists of "models," earnest academic workers can only teach and write as they have learned to think. Here is an examination question about Chaucer for undergraduates at a leading university:

Would an action model (e.g. Teun Van Dijk's or Gerald Prince's) more accurately disclose the narrative structure in "The Knight's Tale" than the satellite/kernel model (e.g. Seymour Chatman's *via* Roland Barthes)? You may offer another view of narrative, e.g. Leo Bersani's or Peter Brooks's psychoanalytic "projections."

When it comes to scholarly publications, the tenor is the same. Here are typical titles from a university-press catalogue: *Toward a Freudian Theory of Literature: With an Analysis of Racine's* Phèdre; *Fetishism & Imagination: Dickens, Melville, Conrad*; *The Corporeal Self: Allegories of the Body in Melville and Hawthorne*; *Melville's Thematics of Form* (poor Melville! like Saint Sebastian he is the target of all the arrows of all the methods); *The Representation of Women in Fiction*; *The Romantic Mother: Narcissistic Patterns in Romantic Poetry*. A recurrent aim is well expressed in a scholar's description of one more book, *Swift's Landscape*: "This profoundly revisionary study forces a major reassessment of the entire conception of landscape as it relates to eighteenth-century literature and aesthetic theory."

These words apply to thousands of these books—they are profoundly revisionary and we must reassess. Reassess what? Some previous theory known to a handful of academics. And what does the theory deal with in this case—literature? No; the conception of landscape in eighteenth-century aesthetic theory. This conception is an idea that somebody derived by analysis from poems and other writings. It did not exist before. One is entitled to doubt whether it is in the poems; it was not in their author's minds—they had only the sight or memory of actual landscapes; and if not in the poem or the mind, then it was not in the eighteenth century either.

In other words, the material of modern scholarship is by now not even the work itself but a curious kind of facsimile, an offprint made up for methodic purposes. What students get is this abstract duplicate and little else. One might say that they disport themselves in this or that "approach" and never reach the real thing. We all know how strongly systems and terminology appeal to the young, and we can guess how much pressure is exerted by a teacher's doctrine and the implied demand for its regurgitation in examinations. Any mental finesse that the graduate or undergraduate student might bring to the work lies dormant or is diverted to the minutiae of analytic methodism.

But what did universities accomplish in times past? It will not do to idealize those times. Schools and universities have never been efficient institutions and they should be judged by their aims and arrangements rather than by their results, which depend so much on the coincidence of a true teacher with an apt student. There is an important clue to past assumptions about culture in the autobiography of John W. Burgess, who was one of the two founders of the graduate school in this country. As a youth of eighteen fighting on the Union side in the Civil War, he made up his mind that if he survived he would study laws and governments so as to see whether wars could be averted by knowledge and intelligence.

After college he went to Germany and studied under the historians Mommsen and Ranke, as well as under Helmholtz, the physicist. He came back to teach at Amherst, and in pursuit of his goal went to Paris to look into the workings of the Ecole Libre des Sciences Politiques. Returning to the United States, he joined the law faculty of Columbia College and soon persuaded the trustees to establish a school of political science. The date was 1880; it was the first graduate school in the country. Partly German and partly French in pattern, it had two stated purposes: to train teachers who would also do research and to form the minds of future politicians and civil servants. No nonsense about culture. Consciously or not, Burgess knew that universities had always been and should continue to be centers for the training of professionals, not for the dissemination of culture. He explicitly took it for granted that the applicants for his school would have completed "their study of universal history and general literature."

What did these two phrases mean? *Universal history* meant the outlines of the development of Western civilization since the Greeks, including contacts with Africa and Asia, and the expansion of Europe in America. As for *general literature*, it embraced chiefly the Greek and Roman authors, studied in their own languages, plus some works by the best-known modern authors, English, French, Italian, and German. As a group, these would not be numerous, but they would be the same for everybody, as dictated by current critical opinion. You would find there a preponderance of poets—Shakespeare, Milton, Molière, Racine, Goethe, Schiller, Dante, Petrarch, Ariosto, and Tasso.

So much for the moderns. What *we* would call moderns in 1880—Tennyson and Browning, Dickens and Thackeray—were for reading on one's own. Likewise with the novelists and poets one or two generations back—Fielding, Wordsworth, Coleridge, Byron, Scott, Jane Austen—none of these were classics for classroom use till much later, when the systematic, analytic study of literature got booming. Earlier (and as late as 1750) the Shakespeare Folio was listed in the Yale University library as "a work of diversion"; by 1850 it was taken more solemnly, and thereafter the reading of one of the plays in college was accompanied by a commentary explaining difficult passages and drawing moral lessons. There would be biographical and historical information, and possibly comparisons with the Greek dramatists and references to the poetics of Aristotle. That was all. It amounted to a sort of beginner's workout for reading reflectively, reading with something more than curiosity about the plot, reading for self-cultivation.

The ancient classics were more thoroughly exploited. They were used as models for composition in verse and prose; as materials for comparative grammar and linguistics; as readings in political and social history; as handbooks of moral teaching and worldly wisdom. For the truly educated they served also as a great body of poetry, myth, philosophy, and eloquence. It is relevant to know how all this vanished from the scene. When, in the 1890s, the classical curriculum tried to compete with the sciences by becoming "scientific" too, it signed its own death warrant. From a student of that period (Nicholas Murray Butler), I heard a revealing anecdote. In third-year Greek the philologist-classicist opened the course by saying, "Gentlemen, we shall begin with the most interesting play of Euripides: it contains nearly every exception to the rules of Greek grammar."

Nobody can fail to note in this remark the dire ambiguity of the word *interesting*—the shift from what Euripides intended and the Athenian audience expected to the meaning that *interest* holds for the analytic scholar. Both interests are genuine and legitimate, but they are not the same, and the more abstract rarely leads to the more concrete. This fact might be called the curse of education: I mean the curse of abstracting and systematizing in order to teach. It is characteristic of our age to reduce every human concern to labels and rules and set up a course in it—two courses, ten courses, at which point we have a school, and a dean, a diploma, and a new profession. Everything useful or pleasant must be acquired from a syllabus, which leaves in its wake mostly self-consciousness. What book and theory have done to love and sexuality is notorious: self-consciousness in marital relations and child-rearing has replaced their inherent difficulties with a host of others labeled and classified.

It is not that knowledge is useless or should be disregarded, but, rather, that learning, doctrine, ideology, is not necessarily an addition to knowledge; it is often a retreat from it. In material life, theory guides practice—that is, improves technology. In the arts, theory comes after the fact of original creation and, far from improving future work, usually spoils it by making the artist a self-conscious intellectual, crippled or misled by "ideas." Not everything that is good can be engineered into existence.

How, then, can culture recover spontaneity, free itself from scholarship? The answer is simple but not agreeable to face. At some point the overexpansion of the present scheme will bring it to collapse from its own weight. It will begin to look as futile as it really is. The Alexandrian textualists came to grief; the scholastics of the Middle Ages faded away. Similarly, the forces of fatigue and boredom will do their work to bring on stagnation and decadence, as happened to the Great English universities in the seventeenth and eighteenth centuries. The idea of a university or of scholarship will not die; it will hibernate, and on reawaking will suggest to its renovators the plain duties they should take on.

Scholarship is not indispensable to culture but can serve it in a material way, by bringing order and clarity into the accumulation of valued things. Scholarship can resume its proper role in establishing readable texts, in explaining obscurities and clearing up confusions in any art, in supplying background and context for the works that are difficult because of remoteness in time or place. It is foolish to think that these tasks are for journeyman labor; on the contrary, they require the greatest tact and sensibility; they call for cultivated minds willing to do a certain amount of drudgery for the sake of giving a jewel the setting it deserves.

Whether the decay of one institution will start or follow the reform of its counterparts throughout society is an open question. But other elements in our present so-called cultural activities will surely undergo change also, for culture's sake. Our speech, for example—our prose made up of jargon and pseudotechnical lingo, which ensure a false profundity and a barrier to disproof—will have to be decanted from its mud and restored to the uses of honest communication. Criticism will need an injection of humility—that is, a recognition of its role as ancillary to the arts, needed only occasionally in a temporary capacity. Since the critic exists only for introducing and explaining, he must be readily intelligible; he has no special vocabulary: criticism is in no way a science or a system. And artists too should drop the burden of theorizing and self-justification that has been forced on them for some 180 years and has produced so much ludicrous or pathetic nonsense. In short, pedantry and pretentiousness must be driven out of the republic of letters.

It remains only to say what good there is in what we have lost. Culture in whatever form—art, thought, history, religion—is for meditation and conversation. Both are necessary sequels to the experience. Cultivation does not come automatically after exposure to the good things as health follows a dose of the right drug. If it did, orchestra players would be the most cultured people musically and copy editors the finest judges of literature. Nor does "reading up" on art suffice unless it spurs meditation and conversation. Both are actions of the mind along the path of finesse. No one can imagine a *systematic* conversation.

As for true meditation, it excludes nothing; its virtue is to comprehend—in both senses: to understand and to take in the fullest view. Both are actions of the mind-and-heart, and therefore charged with the strongest feelings. Indeed, both interior monologue and spoken dialogue aim at discerning which feelings and what degree of each belong to an idea or image. That is how culture reshapes the personality; it develops the self by offering the vicarious experience of art and thought; it puts experience in order.

This active use of time is of course for pleasure; its impulse is love. Everybody used to know this when the words *amateur* and *dilettante* were taken in their original meanings of "lover" and "seeker of delight." We have turned them into terms of contempt to denote bunglers and triflers. But the impulse of love in cultivation leads beyond a selfish pleasure. It leads to communion in two kinds—with the living, by the discovery of kindred spirits in conversation, and with the dead, by the intimacy of admiration for greatness. Today's temper is not conducive to either form of communion. Conversation is wrecked on the shoals of shoptalk, which is factuality unredeemed by thought; and admiration is reproved as uncritical, it being axiomatic that greatness is a myth. The age of the anti-hero sees no warrant for submission to anything or anybody. Yet how, in the absence of this emotion, the fuss we make over art and artists can be justified is not explained.

No doubt the overabundance of works new and old, the multiplicity of things to remember—names, tendencies, schools, and doctrines—cheapens everything and so clutters the memory as to prevent meditation and abort conversation. Faced with the dosage principle of the curriculum, with the good life of That Cosmopolitan Girl, anyone who seeks something more intense has only one avenue of escape, which is the specialism of the single-track connoisseur. In that role he finds approval, self-esteem, and a leisure-time occupation. And he is seconded in his sincere taste by the whole elaborate apparatus of scholarship. The circle is complete; everybody is in the right.

And yet it does not seem as if these well-coordinated arrangements were bringing serenity to the participants. The prevailing mood in this kingdom of analysis, criticalness, and theory is depression. No longer does tragedy purge and exhilarate, nor comedy chastise with gaiety. Music fails to bring calm; painting and sculpture invite chiefly to problem-solving. And I speak not solely of modern works, for our revisionary outlook has by now taken in the whole past. Nietzsche foresaw a hundred years ago the plight of the cultivated mind, whom he embodied in the philosopher:

The spread of the towering sciences has grown enormous and with it the likelihood that the philosopher will grow tired, even as a learner, and will take refuge somewhere and specialize; so that he will no longer reach his proper height—his superspection, circumspection, and "despection." Or he climbs aloft too late, when the best of his maturity and strength are gone, or when he is on the downgrade, coarsened and spoiled; so that his view of the world, his general estimate of things, is no longer of much importance. It is no doubt his intellectual conscience that makes him hesitate to be a dilettante, a centipede, a creature with a thousand antennas.

No scheme lasts forever. There will arise a generation whose "general estimate of things" will regain importance, whose intellectual conscience will impel them in the other direction, toward sensing the world through a thousand antennas. For the bearers of culture continue to be born; the desire for culture is innate. To reincarnate Nietzsche's philosopher, we need only look to the touching figure of the water boy who rowed Dr. Johnson and Boswell down the Thames to Greenwich. The friends were discussing the shaping influence of classical culture. Boswell thought people got on very well without it. Johnson partly agreed. "For instance," he said, "this boy rows us as well without learning as if he could sing the song of Orpheus to the Argonauts, who were the first sailors." Then he interrupted himself and called to the boy: "What would you give, my lad, to know about the Argonauts?" "Sir," said the boy, "I would give what I have."

The Insoluble Problem: Supporting Art

In the beginning, art was the handmaid of religion. Temples, statues of the gods, rituals involving poetry, music, and dance form the cradle of the several arts. When the city is also the whole state, and the citizens all belong to one religion, which is a worship of the city's particular gods, the question of who shall pay for the arts does not arise. Religion, art, public office, and military service are duties that all citizens perform or pay for collectively.

In the course of time, the governors may begin to fancy more secular works, to display the power and greatness of the city. These are again paid for out of public money, sometimes in rather shady ways. For example, Pericles, for the beautification and fortification of Athens, raided the treasury of the Delian League, a defense organization of two hundred city-states. Would that our European allies could be brought to pay for our urban renewal! In the city-state, some citizens develop a wish to enjoy one or another of the arts at home. They pay for this like any other luxury. But in ancient days they had an important advantage: the craftsmen who made the art were not a separate group dependent on commissions for a living: they were slaves, already fully supported, already making pots and pans and other products of artistic skill. (In Egypt, the workmen on public works were not legally slaves, but common people doing forced labor by law.)

23

To the ancient craftsman, the main concern was technique. Art in our sense of aesthetic significance was a by-product, not conscious and purposeful, as is shown by the fact that the better the craftsman, the more he tried to repeat his previous piece of work. This was not true in literature, of course, where interest depended on a degree of novelty, but even there forms and themes tended to be sacrosanct.

The ancients did single out certain artists for admiration, but again it was for their technique; appreciation did not change the common view of their low status as men who worked with their hands. They were not considered educated and were not discussed as particularly important individuals. The craftsmen themselves were interested enough in their techniques to write books about such things as the proportions of the human body or how to use color, and some must have developed an artist's conscious sense of power over something other than matter. But of books about artists there were none until the Hellenistic Period, when a pupil of a pupil of Aristotle's compiled the *Lives of Painters and Sculptors*. Only fragments of it survive, and they suggest that it was anecdotal rather than historical or critical; no such literature about the fine arts arose in antiquity.

As for private patronage in these conditions, the only arrangement that might deserve the name was the latter-day Athenian custom of expecting a wealthy man to give a large sum for the training of the chorus in the annual festival of drama—one day a year when a trilogy and a comedy, both with music and dance, were given free for the whole people. But it appears that to be such a patron was a privilege for which there were more than enough applicants; the festival was never in danger of being canceled.

After the decline of the ancient civilizations, the place and function of art remained the same. Religion was the main motif; the producers were no longer slaves, or even serfs, but still workmen, artisans, usually organized in guilds and supported under uniform rules of pay. When, in late cathedral building, a foreign city called on a successful architect, he went, like a modern contractor, with his team of workers in various arts.

The private customers for art in the Middle Ages made use of these craftsmen as antiquity had done, and the medieval principles of the just price and guaranteed quality meant that competition and artistic rivalry were suppressed by rule and custom. Indeed, the powerful bourgeois class of the High Middle Ages were the ruling power in the towns where they and the craftsmen both lived, so that anything like the modern situation of a free market in which a crowd of artists try to be more popular or better paid than their fellows was inconceivable.

For more than two thousand years, then, church and state—often indistinguishable from each other—were for the arts both impresario and purchaser. They were at times seconded by the wealthy who wanted pieces of art for private use, whether religious or secular, this demand being fulfilled by their social inferiors. To put it another way, all the arts were regarded as practical arts, produced for purposes universally understood. A new style of architecture was not so much an aesthetic innovation as a new feat of engineering.

A notable feature of this outlook and this mode of subsidy is that nobody was likely to enter protests. No middle-class Egyptian trader in figs was heard to say, "To my mind, the pyramid of Cheops is much too squat for beauty." When one of the spires of Chartres cathedral was rebuilt after a fire, its being made in a totally different style from the remaining spire elicited no editorial in the *Chartres Evening Trumpet*. There was no newspaper to assail the decision of the ecclesiastical authorities, no public opinion gathering to petition the mayor. The townsmen had few if any conscious aesthetic ideas; rather, they were proud to have a spire in the latest fashion, with a graceful, fretted outline. Their contribution toward it—pennies or pounds—had gone to the church, not to art directly, and the available money was not fought for by a dozen groups. As to the art itself, it was free of competing "schools," with leaders, doctrines, academic critics, and daily reviewers. Any arguments were private, ephemeral, and did not affect policy or professional careers.

It is with the end of medieval society, marked by a shift in the position of the church and by the formation of national states, that the question Who shall pay for art? arises and proves insoluble. This shift occurred gradually during the three hundred years from 1350 to 1650, which bear the names of Renaissance and Reformation. The Renaissance by its new interests developed individualism; the Protestant Reformation by its renewed search for God encouraged it, while at the same time denouncing the ritualism that had provided so steady a demand for art. In parallel, the rise of nation-states, often at the expense of independent towns, destroyed the link between a small community and its artisans. Add the decay of serfdom and of guilds, and you set the stage for the solitary *artist*, a new social species, who becomes an egotistical wanderer in search of a patron.

From the beginning of that time of transformation we see the rise of cultural diversity, of pluralism and conscious innovation. In Renaissance Italy, a dozen schools of art flourish, soon followed by different ones in Germany, France, and the Netherlands. The artists attach themselves to princes, to popes, to wealthy bourgeois patrons no longer bound by old ideas of just price. We begin to know artists by name, and learn of their tribulations, as we do not—or rarely—know the names and lives of medieval artists. We assign rank and degrees of greatness to these Renaissance men, and so did their contemporaries. The artists themselves become aware of their powers in a new way and their motives in pursuing their craft enlarge, because the artistic *motifs* are no longer concentrated on religious and civic purposes. Art remains propaganda, of course, and ostentation is still at work, but they are now acknowledged as explicit secular acts. And propaganda takes many directions other than pious and ethical; it becomes political and intellectual.

Not that religion had perished in Europe; on the contrary, it had taken a new lease of life with Protestantism and its sequel, the purification of the Roman Church called Counter-Reformation. This double movement affected the patronage of art in curious and unexpected ways. With the stiffening of doctrine on both sides, and actual war leading to the religious division of Europe, it came about that the Protestant courts patronized writers and scholars but not artists; while the Catholic courts, often guided by Jesuits, commissioned the building of churches, tombs, and votive offerings. One type of architecture, indeed, came to be known as the *style jésuite.*

But it was the kings ruling the large, recently unified nations that set the new form of official patronage, for it was they who needed the propaganda of art to give luster to their reign, to associate monarchy with civilization. They gathered at their court: painters, sculptors, architects, poets, musicians, dramatists, choreographers, *plus* a historian or two to make sure the artistic largess was recorded for posterity. Like their predecessors—the Italian princes and popes—the kings managed to get a lot of good work done, and in the course of it established the custom that a great nation owes it to itself to support culture. Opera, ballet, and the theatre, academies for literature, scholarship, and the sciences, soon became a function of the state rather than of the taste or ulterior motive of the person who occupied the throne. This relation still obtains to a greater or lesser degree in modern democracies and even in totalitarian regimes.

But state support differed in kind from the ancient civic support of the arts. First, it exacted a human cost. True, the developed individuality of the artist was no longer cramped by exclusive service to the city and its gods, but as obedience to these impersonal forces was relaxed, obedience to the demands (often the whims) of the patron became compulsory—and galling. One has only to read the autobiography of Benvenuto Cellini to discover how in the High Renaissance a successful artist felt about his many imperious patrons, always resenting the subservient role, meager pay, and likelihood of not getting paid at all.

On their side, artists asserted their independence by maddening slowness in carrying out their commissions and sometimes by never finishing the promised work. The patron lost his temper and often his money given in advance.

Besides, as the state system enlarged the scale of operations, the patron king had to rely on his officials to choose the artists and direct the work. This let in politics and intrigues. For example, Richelieu, acting for Louis XIII, asked François Sublet de Noyers to invite Poussin to come to Paris from Rome, where Poussin, happy and productive, wanted to stay. For a year and a half he put off accepting. Then he got a threatening letter reminding him that he was a French subject and that kings had a long reach. He complied and was well received, but found that the king and the court wanted him as much to snub the popular painter of the town, Vouet, as to produce works of art. And those works were to be large allegorical paintings, no doubt because Poussin had made his reputation with small pastoral scenes. He was, in addition, to design decorations for a long gallery of the Louvre, though he had never worked at architectural decoration. Meantime, the Vouet followers began conspiring to make life hard for this intruder. He endured his troubles for a few months, then escaped back to Rome, on the plea that he must fetch his wife. What Poussin painted in Paris are the least attractive of his works.

The result of this cat-and-dog relation between powerful patron and self-aware artist was not invariable. Rubens was of cheerful temper and he prospered with most of his patrons. But then, he was a born diplomat and a good businessman, qualities that cannot be expected of every artist. The rule is, rather, that in its obsessive drive to create, talent no less than genius is ill-equipped to defend its interests—whence half its miseries.

The other half comes from envious rivals and the traits of the patrons themselves. The famous cases are typical—Mozart's mistreatment by the Archbishop of Salzburg; Beethoven's grievances, right or wrong, against his titled friends in Vienna; La Bruyère's need for incessant self-control in the brutish ducal house of Condé. Even the easygoing Haydn suffered and complained, and if Velásquez got on well with Philip IV of Spain, it was not solely because he could paint admirable portraits; it was also because he took care of the king's apartments, supervising janitors, buying supplies, and doing menial chores. In short, good patrons and amiable artists come together even more rarely than perfectly matched spouses.

By the 1700s, moreover, "art" and "artist" had subtly acquired new meanings. The good or great artist was now understood to possess more than high technical competence, and he had gradually come to feel a special kind of self-regard. The graphic artists particularly demanded freedom of action; when commissioned they would no longer tolerate being told "don't change or add anything." They had become "inventors" and in a couple of centuries would be called "creators." Genius at first meant ingenuity; later it meant superhuman powers.

This transformation, naturally, was not instantaneous or uniform. The ancient slave and the medieval wage earner had disappeared, but the social status of the newly risen artist was indefinite—an embarrassment to all: at times he was the companion of princes, at another moment, he was classified with bricklayers and upholsterers. Part of the uncertainty was due to the surviving ideal of the Renaissance man, which called for gentlemen to be broadly educated in science, art, and liberal learning, and thereby encouraged kings and courtiers themselves to write poetry, play music, and even act and dance in court theatricals. But could the king dance with a ballet master; should a gentleman publish poetry?

A further complication arose when, side by side with royal and state patronage, two or three other sources of support became prominent. One was the purchase of art by wealthy amateurs. A tax farmer such as Fouquet rivaled Louis XIV in expenditure and taste, and thereby earned his downfall. But he was imitated on a smaller scale by many of his class, and the habit of buying art took hold among the higher bourgeoisie. It was in fact a return to the medieval ways, before the towns were eclipsed by monarchs and princes. But now the middle class had no local guild workers to command. They had to commission Franz Hals or Rembrandt to paint those group portraits commemorating officership in the militia. They ordered engravers to reproduce these works, sculptors to make busts or crucifixes, and of course architects to design houses and gardens. Some, like the mid-eighteenth-century music lover La Popelinière in Paris, treated themselves to a private orchestra.

Repeated bargaining between artists and patrons who were or had been merchants was bound to turn the pair into regular buyers and sellers. The relation differs from that between the king or the pope and Benvenuto Cellini, who would ask for the cost of his materials and then receive a reward, an unstated prize for his work. The era of haggling, of high-, medium-, and low-priced art was beginning. It led, of course, to the open market situation we take for granted today. The market had long been the source of support for the theatre, and by the middle of the eighteenth century it became the main support of literature. Pope is said to have been the first English writer to make a living by his pen alone. But lordly patrons continued to play their role; they were very useful for launching a work by subscription and absolutely necessary for obtaining a sinecure. This last form of state patronage was reserved for writers, who would be expected to praise the patron in dedications, defend him and his politics in pamphlets, or tutor his children and take them on the grand tour.

These new means of sustaining art turned the artist from a domestic, a courtier, or a "favorite" into an independent entrepreneur, a dealer-manager-advertiser of his own wares. By the nineteenth century, this situation, combined with the evils of industrialization, brought on the open conflict between the artist and society that has characterized the last 150 years.

Two contrary movements made this conflict inevitable and permanent. One was the glorification of art as the highest spiritual expression of man's life on earth. The artist-genius thereby became a seer and a prophet. He knew and proclaimed the ultimate truths that condemned the materialism of everyday life; he denounced the world, flouted its rules of behavior, and also foretold the march of culture, because he was leading it—whence the term *avant-garde.* This view of society was confirmed by the hostile response of his contemporaries. They were the philistines, born enemies of everything fine and noble; for they were part of the opposite movement of the century, utilitarian, bent on material progress and social stability. War between the two was declared by the very act of creating unconventional art; no peace was possible, because the aims of the two sides were irreconcilable. It was the prophet and the saint against the compact majority of sinners. The contempt automatically attached today to the term *bourgeois* has its source and its expression in the arts of the nineteenth century.

That the rebels who produced this art were for the most part sons and daughters of the bourgeoisie made the attacks even more venomous: there are no fiercer quarrels than those within the family. That in the end each philistine generation came to understand and admire made no difference. That even before the belated or posthumous consecration some patrons had been helpful and the state had given subsidies made no difference either. Too many of these opportunities favored artists who were indeed competent, but only as imitators, not innovators. Thus arose the now common distinction between art and academic art.

In the midst of this unceasing battle at the core of society, a peculiar institution developed. It was called Bohemia, a self-defined district in the poorer part of a capital city, where artists from all over gravitated and formed a community that was congenial because of the denizens' similar habits and shoptalk, and because life was much cheaper there than on the "respectable" side of town. In Bohemia, the unsung patrons of art might be a landlady, a small-restaurant owner, a secondhand-bookseller; they gave food, shelter, cash or credit to their favorites, often without a thought of being repaid.

Our century has inherited and supplemented the tutti-frutti of patronage. The nineteenth century may be said to have ended in 1914, and after the murderous war that began then, Western societies had changed. For one thing, it looked as if the philistine had been killed along with the other millions. For another, the newest art was more than ever a criticism of life and a refuge from its horrors. By 1920 art as such was the concern or pastime of a wider public than ever before, and, no matter how weird its latest forms, was accepted without protest. The past had shown that the public was always wrong, so wisdom and snobbery alike dictated humble submission to whatever came. For these philistines in reverse gear everything in a gallery or a book or on the stage was "interesting." It was experimental, and who would dare to challenge an experiment? Authority had passed from the customer-patron to the supplier-artist.

During the great upheaval, many of the old fortunes had disappeared and the upper classes had forfeited their prestige and power. To make up for these changes, the state was called upon to enlarge its role as patron. It must set up a ministry of culture and see to it that the people received their due portion of art and the creators their reward. Art was too important to be left to the whims of a ruling class. The whole nation must be aestheticized; the schools from the earliest years must initiate the love and practice of the arts, encourage young talent. Even England broke its laissez-faire tradition and, besides a National Theatre, set up an Arts Council.

So much for Europe. It was left to the United States to innovate most lavishly. It improvised three new kinds of patron: the private foundation, the private corporation, the private university. As a teacher, performer, and supporter of art, the American university is still unique. It fell into its new role when the Americans who had gone to Paris after the First World War returned in the thirties with a new outlook on life, including a taste for foreign food and high art. They made disciples rapidly, causing a spate of amateur and professional works that the market could not absorb. The country was in depression, and for the first time in the United States, government came to the rescue of starving artists.

When recovery came, these gifted people infiltrated the academy. Colleges and universities created art departments, built theatres, captured revolving poets, stationary stage directors, and composers-in-residence; they turned the glee club into a chorus and orchestra, set up film units, attached a string quartet to the faculty—in short, became recruits of the world-wide sect of art-as-religion. Its influence after one generation could be read in the manifesto of the rioting students at Chicago in 1968; two of their demands were: the abolition of money and every man or woman an artist.

Meanwhile, the American corporation had come to the view that it was an institution with social duties to discharge. One way was through contributions to charity and education, and soon also to the arts. What is more, by the 1950s, company directors were buying for their boardrooms and reception halls paintings and sculptures that they ultimately came to like. Today, one reads that Merrill Lynch or IBM is sponsoring a large exhibition and that the Pepsi-Cola Art Collection is once more on its travels to show the world that Americans are no longer barbarians.

Third and last, of the many private foundations that are also peculiar to the United States, a great many include or specialize in the support of art, both its making and its performance. In tandem, Washington and the states have set up the National Endowment and the arts councils.

Under a wide sweep of the eye, art partonage in the Western world looks as if it had corrected its past defects and achieved a satisfactory system of support. Not relying solely on the wealthy and powerful, it is organized for fair competition among talents; it combines public and private money; it is enthusiastically sustained and, in a sense, supervised by public opinion; and it supplements a large and free economic market that is itself organized and permanent: dealers, galleries, publishers, editors, recording companies, museums, libraries, and theatres are regular customers or conduits for purchase money from eager buyers. Is all this not adequate and admirable?

Admirable it certainly is in intention, and it refutes the cliché about a wholly materialistic society. But adequate it is not—neither to the supply of art nor to the practical and emotional demands of artists and their well-wishers. For what has developed in step with these arrangements is a tremendous growth in the output of art, propelled as it is by unremitting social encouragement and individual ambition. The religion of art has so many adherents that every unit in society longs to join in artistic expression; school, church, and town; businesses, hospitals, and cruise vessels—all want to be art centers. Meantime, from infancy onward, every spark of talent is blown into a flame by the breath of universal approval.

The upshot is that everywhere well-trained individuals and groups clamor for support; everywhere grant applications are being filled out; everywhere art institutions are in deficit; everywhere, the faithful public continues to pay prices close to exorbitant; and everywhere the art community—patrons and producers—is outraged at a situation it thinks intolerable: all this wealth of talent and no wealth of money! Where can some be had? Fund-raising, of course. Thus the scramble for subsidy grows fiercer as a double inflation presses upon the total patronage fund—the common inflation in costs and the inflation of ever more individual artists, more groups and centers and festivals.

Can the present agencies do better? The obstacles seem insurmountable. Consider:

First. It is hard to imagine any new source of money that would provide a further infusion into the pool of patronage.

Second. The welfare nations have other burdens—the poor and the aged, the schools and the health apparatus, the unemployed and the retired. Public funds cannot be stretched indefinitely for the arts.

Third. Private patrons are few, and many foundations are winding up their programs, by design or under legal compulsion.

Fourth. The colleges and universities have reached their capacity to provide support. Enrollments are down and costs are up; teaching positions are filled. Further, demographic reports show a diminishing birthrate, which precludes a surge in enrollments and fresh resources.

Fifth. The popular arts are competing more and more successfully with high art, not indeed for patronage—the popular arts pay their way—but for public interest at a high level. They take money and attention from the other kind of art.

Sixth. The desperate shifts used by museums, libraries, and churches, such as renting out space for cocktail parties or filmmaking; the retail merchandising of goods; the program series of music, theatre, and other performances; the "voluntary" levy at the door of a hitherto free public institution, have begun to alienate the public. It resents the bazaar atmosphere and the unfair competition with the other purveyors of art struggling in the marketplace.

So much for the financial side. Now for the claims of art:

First. Perpetual poverty is disheartening, undignified, and contrary to the public's own estimate of art. Artists do not go out of business if their goods do not sell; they keep producing even if they starve. Art institutions are rescued, yearly, partly, at the last minute, and continue their precarious existence. This wretchedness creates the impression of miserly patronage.

Second. There is no conceivable device for limiting overproduction. No zoning laws can be enacted against art, no Malthusian spirit instilled into the artists. Nor can the public be persuaded that its heedless encouragement of would-be artists is cruel. The life of art—no regular hours; no boss; self-expression, with ego at a premium; praise for scorning the common material goals—remains attractive to the young and they enter the scrimmage with high hopes.

Third. Young or old, artists view both the market and the patrons as alien forces to be repeatedly conquered. They come to hate the rules of the trade and the life of grantsmanship. Rejected applicants despise the quasi-official style, the art that is "safe." They idealize the days of popes and kings.

Fourth. The public is assailed by so much art that it unconsciously protects itself against it. One way is the star system. Headliners save thinking, but they also constitute a kind of monopoly to the detriment of the large and less successful majority.

Fifth. The glut leads to a second protective response. The experience of high art becomes commonplace and loses its intensity. Instead of being enthralled participants, the followers of art turn placid consumers. Arts councils and foundation officials are especially susceptible to this attrition of feeling, which means that awards rarely go to original workers. Geniuses run the same risk of lifelong neglect as they always did.

In short, an extraordinarily bountiful and many-sided system gives rise to continual and *justified* complaint. No earlier scheme, as we saw, has proved satisfactory either. And to redesign ours would mean a series of impossibilities that can be summed up as deliberate discouragement: of the young artistic impulse, of the mature desire for a public career, of the competitive scramble at the great centers. It seems as if high art were from the beginning under a curse that grows more bitter as civilization spreads ever wider the demand for a good that it produces all too abundantly.

Look It Up! Check It Out!

In advanced civilizations the period loosely called Alexandrian is usually associated with flexible morals, perfunctory religion, populist standards and cosmopolitan tastes, feminism, exotic cults, and the rapid turnover of high and low fads—in short, a falling away (which is all that decadence means) from the strictness of traditional rules, embodied in character and enforced from within.

But another sign of such times is: reference books. The old civilization has piled up works of the mind for centuries—the attic is crammed full—and direct access to the treasures grows less easy, less frequent, as the social revolution brings more and more of the untaught and the self-indulgent out of bondage. At that point the museum is born, and the research library. There, the inmates—scholars and specialists—begin to digest, organize, theorize, and publish reference books. The term *Alexandrian* comes from the famous establishment of this sort—the *Mouseion*, the Muses' library and scholar's hostel, at Alexandria in the third century B.C.

Alexandrianism comes in various sizes: lesser ones can be followed by vigorous returns to discipline, firsthand knowledge, and creativeness, as happened at the tail end of the Middle Ages and again at the turn of the eighteenth century. Similarly, a healthy barbarian invasion may clear the air and the bookshelves for a fresh start. But during the very pleasant time of relaxed mental life through culture from handbooks, nobody can tell what is to happen next. Today, judging solely by the output of reference books, one

37

would say that our Alexandrianism was of the largest dimensions since Alexandria itself.

Just try to count the guides to single subjects, from poetry and gastronomy to witchcraft and world myths; the "companions" to world literatures; the "encyclopedias of modern culture"; the tremendous Scribner series of reading-reference works that digest in single chapters the lives and works of writers from Homer to Pinter, or that survey such large subjects as American Diplomatic History, Shakespeare, and the civilizations of East Asia.

The shelves creak under the collections of facts and extracts: of book reviews, biographies, quotations—general, medical, legal, humorous, biographical, classical, and foreign. With *Literary* (and, later, *Legal*) *Anecdotes*, the Oxford Press has opened a new series of tidbits, to which an excellent *Aphorisms* by John Gross was soon added. We also have lists of everything—of books, naturally, but also of authors, artists, abbreviations, museums, as well as of portraits, nicknames, fictional characters, mammals, and former U.S. governors. The Gale Research Company publishes in many volumes excerpts of literary criticism from the earliest times to last week. Finally, with the computer and its capacity for classifying and regurgitating has come the blind fury of compilation. Innumerable repertories appear, each ostensibly useful to some researcher—and what person capable of reading is not today a researcher, by necessity, accident, or choice?

The Alexandrian outlook includes one other important subject of concern: language. Studying texts soon turns the searchlight from ideas to words, after which language as a whole seems to hold the secret of all the great questions. Many otherwise sober persons tell us that language is the shaping force of poems and plays; philosophers argue that usage analyzed will answer the riddles of Being; and even scientists turn verbalist when they speak of a genetic "code" or account for disease by supposing "information" to be carried hither and yon by cells or molecules. Information theory, not interested in message, but in the chances of getting its "shape" across, tries to dominate psychology, linguistics, and anything else in which meaning still lurks untouched by abstraction. The point of the game is what we all used to do as children—repeat a word over and over till its meaning is emptied out.

We need only look at some dictionaries and other books about words. Besides the well-known for everyday use in the home, the college, and the office, there are hundreds of others that profess to throw light on language, whether to improve writing and guide usage or to spur the love of words, to encourage verbal playfulness and tickle curiosity, or simply to record. In bulk, they suggest heroic patience and pertinacity: the first volume of *DARE* has just appeared, that is, *The Dictionary of American Regional English*, a monumental project that has been under way for generations.

So much compiling and disseminating of data in small bundles is, among other things, an orgy of self-consciousness. We seem to live mainly in order to see how we live, and this habit brings on what might be called the externalizing of knowledge; with every new manual there is less need for its internal, visceral presence. The owner or user feels confident that he possesses its contents—there they are, in handy form on the handy shelf. And with their imminent transfer to a computer, that sense of possession will presumably attach itself to the hard disk or the phone number of the data bank.

To say this is also to say that the age of ready reference is one in which knowledge inevitably declines into information. The master of so much packaged stuff has less need to grasp context or meaning than his forebears: he can always look it up. His active memory is otherwise engaged anyway, full of the arbitrary names, initials, and code figures essential to carrying on daily life. He can be vague about the rest: he can always check it out.

For still greater comfort, there are people everywhere whose sole job in life is to look it up and check it out. I mean the researchers and verifiers on the staffs of periodicals, publishers, broadcasting stations, government bureaus, and private agencies of every sort, whether promoting a cause or monitoring a menace. No doubt these earnest minds know something in the ancient sense, but it is only a small part of what they look up and check out and send forth as true. Much of their work we receive free and unsolicited, in print or otherwise, whereby our sense of boundless horizons presumably grows apace. But what we are experiencing is not the knowledge explosion so often boasted of; it is a torrent of information, made possible by first reducing the known to compact form and then bulking it up again—adding water. That is why the product so often tastes like dried soup.

At the same time, an uneasy feeling attends this loss of the concrete, and it may be for this reason that so much has been written about words. The aim is to help out writers presumably educated and intellectual. What appears strange is that no encouraging result is noticeable. Perhaps this failure is due to the tone and quality of the books themselves. Let us look at a few.

The most Alexandrian of the works offered to us is *The Wordtree* by Henry G. Burger, a quarto of 380 closely packed pages, described as "A Transitive Cladistic for Solving Physical and Social Problems." According to the author, the volume serves this purpose by analyzing a quarter-million words: it "branches them binarily to pinpoint the concepts . . . to produce a handbook of physical and social engineering."

How this magic is accomplished, the compiler tells us, is through the pairing of ideas with their causes and effects as these are embodied in words. Roget's familiar *Thesaurus* gives only synonyms and associates; the user has to choose among them according to his sense of nuance. In the interlocking vocabulary of *The Wordtree*, the user is guided toward terms of process and procedure, antonyms and alternatives, and kindred sorts of linkage. Not that this labyrinth is easy to enter. In addition to some fifty abbreviations (rather poorly devised), there are a dozen symbols, whose position or combination signifies connections said to be factual. The rest of the interweaving relies on reference by number from an Index to a

Hierarchy. To master the system it is necessary to study fifty pages of explanation.

One can readily see the appeal of the scheme to its maker: words stand for ideas and acts; these have multiple bonds relating them to practical life and speculative thought. Therefore a map of the network could be used to clarify both thought and action. The task of making this map, we are told, took twenty-seven years, and even so some areas in it are "underdeveloped" but being worked on.

With all due respect to this industry and ingenuity, two objections occur at once to the claim of practical utility. One is that a mind capable of threading the maze which is this book would be capable of reaching the same results unaided. The "social engineering" it hopes to facilitate may well begin with clear notions of cause and effect or some other sequence, but that first step presents difficulties only to those who would never be able to use *The Wordtree*.

The second objection is that the "hierarchy" of words and acts is unavoidably full of misfits, because language is not made up of rigid interlocking parts. Its very power to serve thought depends on the flexibility that results from its waywardness. For example, on the very first page of instructions, which is also the endpaper, we are shown the connections of the word *Plan*. Through its first link, *maneuver*, we find the statement that "maneuver *causes* (or at least enables) . . . a pushover or a utopia." A social engineer would be ill-advised to maneuver in the expectation of either one.

Since occasional flaws do not discredit a large work, especially in its first edition, it is only fair to test it further. A sampling shows the same dismaying results, together with a surprising unpracticality in the choice of terms. Where is the utility of such verbs as *to superordinate, to readprotect, to julienne, to disembargo, to disgovern, to adjustify, to naphthalize, to semicastrate*? Is this the language of social action—these negatives, compounds, and half measures?

One test of the proffered "cause and effect" was suggested to me by the news that the work on the ceiling of the Sistine Chapel was now open to view. What does *The Wordtree* offer on *restore*? The first equivalents are: *change* and *normalize*, followed by a list of words supposedly parallel to *change*: *"dimpled* (dimp), *fallowed* (barefallow), *galleted* (taliacotify), *healed* (recuperate), *remedied* (therapize), *modernize* (renovize)." This last pair is preceded by a sign that directs us to combine ideas in the form: *"to* change *and also to* modernize means to renovize." Why *renovate* nowhere appears is a mystery, but let it pass. It is these combinings ("binary" to ape computer science) that fatally ruin the scheme. We learn, as a guiding example, that "to maneuver and to govern is to gerrymander." Really, it won't do, any more than *campaign* usefully goes with both *strategy* and *periodize*, the latter being elsewhere linked with (the so far unheard-of) *strategied*.

In short, here is Alexandrianism destroying in its devotee both the feeling for language and the judgment of practical affairs. One may say this in spite of what Conrad Arensberg, the distinguished Columbia anthropologist, says in his foreword to the book about its being "on the right track, scientifically, historically, and humanistically . . . a contribution to anthropological science and to lexicography itself." Anthropological and humanistic are precisely the qualities that manuals and digests do not possess, some because of their nature—for example, a table of logarithms—others, such as this "tree" of notions, because in spite of their humanistic substance, their compilers have handled it like would-be scientists.

Among the Alexandrian aids to users of words, many make no pretence to scholarship. They address the general reader and one detects in them the humanist impulse. Their purpose might be described as general hoopla for language. For example, in *Our Marvelous Native Tongue*; *Words, Words, Words*; *Words About Words*; *World of Words*; the laconic *Words*, and Leo Rosten's *Hooray for Yiddish!*, the authors act as cheerleaders bent on arousing the stolid to share the writers' own enthusiasm.

Next comes a subclass, the Improvers. They range from guides to usage (e.g., the late Wilson Follett and the compilers of *The Harper Dictionary of Contemporary Usage*) to the inditers of manuals for better writing (the famous Strunk and White, William K. Zinsser, Rudolf Flesch) and the special watchmen, who warn against such dangers as deceptive words, native, British, and foreign. This group of books is very large but again, judging from current writing, mostly without effect. Or perhaps one should say that they help sustain the good writing that is done, though powerless to amend the bad. In any case, one remembers with shame that the great Elizabethan and Augustan writers did not even have dictionaries.

The failure of all this well-meant help is due in part to its poor quality. The mentors repeat futile advice in chummy tones: "Don't be afraid of rules!" "Write short sentences," as if the difficult craft of brevity were a cure for nonsense and malaprops. Some mislead about diction, too. For example, the large *Dictionary of Euphemisms and Other Doubletalk* blurs distinctions right and left, sarcastically pointing out "the truth." Thus *"direct mail*: unsolicited mail or, descending one more notch toward reality, junk mail." We learn that *homicide* is a genteelism for *murder* and *illegal* for *criminal*—as if manslaughter were not also homicide and illegality broader than crime. By the same bent of mind, *document, fatigue, fib, incident, journalist, miscarriage, nurse* (verb), *party* (noun), *portly, questionable, seat belt*, and many other words are declared euphemisms, which the spade-a-spade brigade would have us replace by more honest terms: the author thinks *upchuck* should be *vomit* and *streetwalker* should be *prostitute.*

Regarding another element of style, teachers of Latin have a point when they remind us that an acquaintance with "their" language would help us with ours, but the handbooks so far produced to serve the purpose have been disappointing. *Amo, Amas, Amat and More*, for example, is but a collection of Latin tags and maxims, with pronunciation, translation, and a quick comment added. It is supposed to help readers when "plagued by writers and speakers who blithely drop Latin phrases into their English sentences." Why "plagued"? It implies getting rid of the phrases and maxims. For the maxims there are better dictionaries than this: for the phrases (*ex officio, ad lib, bona fide*, etc.) almost any English dictionary will do. For the rest, one wonders where the modern reader will stumble on *magister artis ingeniique largitor venter*? or on *ne supra crepidam sutor iudicaret*? The usual form of the proverb among older writers is terser: *ne sutor ultra crepidam*; so the poor reader remains plagued.

As for the pitfalls of British English, they were well charted a dozen years ago by Norman Schur in *British Self-Taught*, and the more recent *British / American Language Dictionary* by Norman Moss adds little. It is skimpy, full of perishable slang, and often marred by slips and clumsy phrasing (*infiltrated on to*). It fails, moreover, to draw attention to *chat with* (*to*), *cater to* (*for*) and similar divergences, while it disregards large differences: "Billiards: a kind of pool." Truly, our would-be crutches are broken reeds.

The main reason why so much advice leads to so little bettering is that the cultural current flows not toward the simple and lucid but the other way, toward the novel and singular at any price. The democratic temper is not less pedantic than the Alexandrian. Modern poets and novelists, aided by advertisers, have shown everybody how to tamper with idiom and meaning and be original by rifling the learned vocabulary. When *metaphor* has come into daily use as a poor synonym for "it reminds me of," one is not surprised to hear that a Senate committee reporting on the CIA thought *synecdoche* would be an apt word for *concealment*. Fortunately, a Washington columnist ridiculed the term out of existence.

But this stroke of sanity is exceptional. The passion for strange ornaments continues and finds support in books that are in essence Special Lists. Of course, a solid piece of work such as *A Dictionary of Soldier Talk*, by three army men, is special without catering in the least to novelty hunting; it is a sober, reliable dictionary. But the subtitles of such books as *The Transitive Vampire: A Handbook of Grammar for the Innocent, the Eager, and the Doomed* indicate the prevailing mood. *A Browser's Dictionary*, by the late John Ciardi, is perhaps the best representative of the genre. The *Browser*, and its sequel, *A Second*, etc. sprang from John Ciardi's wide reading and persistent searching. He relished folk etymologies and the byways of lexicography. His work disputes accepted views and gives reminders of curious origins, e.g., *fornicate*: in architecture, *arched*, from *forno* (oven, furnace). The lower arches of large Roman buildings being places of solicitation, their name was attached first to the prostitute (*fornix*), then to the performance itself. Other entries are more speculative but no less interesting—e.g., to knock *galleywest*, which Mark Twain authenticates. Still others, such as the derivation of *gunsel* from *gun*, are unconvincing: Dashiell Hammett settled that one long ago as a corruption of the German *gänsel*, little goose or young homosexual.

Since poetry and novels in Alexandria must be written in the latest demotic speech, there is need for *The Barnhart Dictionary of New English Since 1963* and *A Dictionary of Contemporary and Colloquial Usage*. A similar need exists for the several dictionaries of slang, American, English, and French, and for bilingual ones linking these in pairs. The rapid turnover of terms in this category suggests that we really ought to have, not a book, but a quarterly, with a section at the back for new acronyms and initialese. As it is, the books show how quickly, in these parts of our literature, meaning perishes. They show also how ambiguous it is from the start. This is obvious in naming objects and institutions by initials only; it is nearly as bad in slang. For example, *funky* is used to mean *cheap, smelly, generally no good, solid, very good, beautiful*.

Such innovative turns also kill many a straight word: now that *tacky* means *shabby* or *badly made*, the sense *sticky, not quite dry* (as of paint) has been shut out. And confusion spreads further through the now established practice of making verbal mongrels and portmanteaus. The new vocabulary includes such forms as *radiothon* and *puritron* for daily use and loftier hybrids for literature. Children may not read Edward Lear and Lewis Carroll any longer, but word play lives on, and adults who encounter Joyce or his imitators will be glad of Myra Livingston's *Learical Lexicon*. It lists words from Lear's letters to his friends, exemplifying all the devices: punning (*phits of coffin*), plain extensions (*begloomed*), portmanteaus (*meloobious*), cockneyisms (*wurble inwentions*) and spelling tricks (*specktickle*). After that, everyone is prepared for all adventures from *Alice* to *Finnegan*.

Reference works on large subjects can serve politics, as the eighteenth-century French encyclopedia was the first to show. Can books about words do the same? The recent revision of Roget's *Thesaurus* to eliminate sex bias from the vocabulary is an attempt to manipulate society through single words. More consecutive, Dennis Baron's *Grammar and Gender* gives an account of the mistreatment of women through language. It is, says he, "a litany of shame," and he discusses the efforts made in our century to invent corrective pronouns and compounds. But he concludes that the English terms at issue have been formed by many influences other than men's biological drive to dominate the other sex. When one learns that some feminists want to replace such words as *history* by *herstory*, one can compliment them on the odd pun but not on their knowledge or prudence. In any case, gender is not sex; the latter is natural, the former notional. In Latin, sailors and poets are feminine in declension; on the continent of Europe, the sun and moon switch gender from one language to another without implications of superior or inferior; in English, both are neuter. And in one African language a woman's breast is feminine if small, masculine if large: it would be foolish to draw political conclusions. Let us reach equity for the sexes on a firmer basis.

The fate of knowledge in a welter of facts was our concern at the start; it claims attention in a new form at the close. For there is no denying that the defects in the books criticized above were due to poor technique. A professional knows at least what others have written and can borrow from their understanding. But professionalism has its drawbacks. To take a notable example, the late Eric Partridge, who produced two masterly works, *Origins* (etymologies) and *Slang and Unconventional English*, showed weak judgment throughout his dictionaries of *Clichés* and of *Catch-Phrases.* He confused clichés with idioms ("hear a pin drop" with "now and then"), and he misinterpreted phrase after phrase in American writers and the older English—he had not read enough *as a reader.* It is the lexicographer's occupational ailment to become a hardware dealer who tosses nuts and bolts into bins, judging by externals only. His method blinds him to the art of words and he misconceives what he calls the life of language.

Whoever is interested in this cold war between the lexicographer or linguist and the writer or veteran reader should follow the publications of the Dictionary Society of North America, whose center is Indiana State University at Terre Haute. Alexandrian in the best sense, these journals enable one to learn much of interest that is being done about words. One sees the criteria for making dictionaries becoming more and more exacting and abstract. One also hears those who develop the rules being pitiless in their arrogance, especially toward writers who believe in right and wrong and who judge by insight and observation instead of research.

Thus a review of John Ciardi's second *Browser* dismissed it as "not worth a second look." And when another writer objected to a badly formed and thoroughly misleading new word, a lexicographer jumped on him with the factual bludgeon that "it had been around a long time"—he had found it in a text thirty years ago. The empirical truth that it was never heard or read in newspapers until the last few months, as a result of world-wide alarm over an unquestionably new disease, did not change the linguist's belief in the antiquity, and hence legitimacy, of the word. This mechanical reliance on a datum is mistaken for objectivity. One recalls the large *Webster*, third edition, in which it is said that many educated Americans throughout the country use *ain't* in casual conversation. The evidence, when tracked down, was a research paper that found half-a-dozen such speakers somewhere in the Middle West.

The evolution of dictionaries is thus from simple utility to elaborate ritual. It began, as we learn from the excellent *History of Foreign Language Dictionaries*, with the ancient Alexandrian's perplexity about unusual Greek words by then no longer understood. Latin was similarly charted in Rome's latter days, and again in the Renaissance. *Dictionaries*, by the noted lexicographer Sidney I. Landau, supplies the matching story of English dictionaries, together with a lucid discussion of the theory behind the latest rules. He laments, for example, that there are no "external criteria" for determining slang. Similarly, the reality of "good usage" (or in linguistic euphemism "standard English"), which rests on the circular argument that that is good which good users use, ulcerates the whole profession. And it is no doubt this expression of pain that makes the literary think lexicographers do not really know what language is.

Perhaps a post-Alexandrian age will decide that to consider words as objects is science misapplied—it is physics, not biology. Nor is language even purely biological, being distinctively human. Meanwhile, it is enheartening to read the splendid account of the making of the *OED*, *Caught in the Web of Words*, by the granddaughter of its great designer, Sir James Murray. That vast enterprise was largely the work of amateurs, of readers coached and coaxed and bullied by a genius whose publishers, the Oxford University Press, did little but badger *him* and dole out meager subsidies. Oxford still thrives on the proceeds of the work, while lexicographers criticize it for not following the rules developed since: expect no justice in Alexandria.

To try to settle the conflict would be foolish as well as futile; it would argue a pathetic ignorance of history, which shows that strife over letter and spirit is unending. Another great Murray, Sir Gilbert, illustrates this truth in his *Religio Grammatici* by quoting the complaint of Isocrates: "The scroll he sends to Philip will not be able to say what he wants it to say, because Philip will hand it to a secretary, and the secretary, neither knowing nor caring what it is all about, will read it out 'with no persuasiveness, no indication of changes of feeling, as if he were giving a list of items.'"

Our reference works are lists, and as we turn the page to check or look up the item, Philip's secretary is reincarnated in our minds. Perhaps a close observer would notice a Greek A glowing faintly on our foreheads.

Where Is History Now?

If a frequency count were taken to find out how often we read or hear the word *history*, the result would suggest that the modern populations are passionately fond of the subject. Newspapers are full of historical "finds"; historical societies and museums are open to the public in towns of every size; "preservation" is ubiquitous—old houses, disused workshops, iron bridges, log cabins are declared forever sacrosanct; Williamsburg and Fort Dearborn are thriving tourist attractions; and the anniversary habit is endemic. Not merely the Constitution, but the founding of businesses, the merger of banks, and the first appearance of magazines are celebrated with equal piety at short intervals. Our collective mind must be steeped in history and insatiable for more.

The conclusion is regrettably untrue. Our pastimes bespeak rather the collecting mania, antiquarian puttering, and the cultivation of nostalgia with bits and pieces of the past. None of these has anything to do with the uses and pleasures of history properly so called. This confusion of ideas was well illustrated when it was announced that the research vessel on which Marconi carried out his experiments with wireless and which had been destroyed in the last war, was to be "re-created." Marconi was said to have "lost a piece of his history." Somehow this absurdity passes muster; it is no longer obvious that Marconi's history cannot have been changed by any later event. The destruction affected only a memento whose "re-creation" is part of *our* history, not his.

History is not a piece of crockery dredged up from the *Titanic*; it is, first, the shipwreck, then a piece of writing. What is more, it is a piece of writing meant to be read, not merely entered on shelves and in bibliographies. By these criteria, modern man must be classed as a stranger to history; he is not eager for it nor bothered by the lack of it. The treasure hunt for artifacts seems to him a sufficient acknowledgment of the past.

To be sure, many books appear under the old label, history, but they usurp the name and actually cater to very different kinds of interest. This fact is made plain in the various modifiers that are used in front of "history"—psycho-, socio-, quanto-history. These variants have come into being under the influence of a group of scholars in France, known as the *Annales* group, from the name of their journal. Their program, inspired by populism, by the rise of the social sciences, by the recurrent hope of a "scientific" history, and by simple boredom with the former ways of historiography, dates back to the turn of the nineteenth century. Although founded in 1929, the governing ideas of the *Annales* were set forth between 1897 and 1903 by Durkheim, Simiand, and others, who shared with the new psychologists the determination to find in their subjects the "deeper" or "essential" features. Hence their disdain for "mere description." The new program would presumably make room for ideas and attitudes in addition to fact and take the historian into the wider stream of life.

It was soon found that many kinds of documents existed, so far untouched and worth exploiting—county archives, private contracts, children's books, records of matriculation at colleges and universities, the police blotter in big cities, gravestones in cemeteries—a whole world of commonplace papers and relics to be organized into meanings. Such documents told nothing important individually; they had to be classified and counted. Theirs was a mass meaning, and it brought one nearer to the life of the people; it satisfied democratic feelings.

The new resolve has produced in the name of history such studies as: *Murdering Mothers: Infanticide in England and New England 1558–1803*; *Poverty and Welfare in Habsburg Spain*; *American*

Collegiate Populations; *Madness, Anxiety, and Healing in 17th Century England*; *Fluctuations in the Prosperity of a Cloth-Making Town in Languedoc 1633–1789*; *A Prison of Expectations: The Family in Victorian Culture*. And from the disciples of "depth" psychology: *White Racism: A Psychohistory*.

When one looks closer, one sees that these works rely on the sampling method—*Poverty in Habsburg Spain* has the subtitle: "The Example of Toledo." The prison which is marriage (or marriage which is prison) is depicted through the lives of five Victorian novelists. The madness and anxiety study is an analysis of the work of one astrologer-physician with a large practice. Notice, too, the time limits, as narrow as the scope: the accounts of infanticide and the cloth-making prosperity end, the one in 1803, the other in 1789. The evidence is still narrower. One must take Toledo for Spain and five (unusual) marriages for all others. The reader who happens to want history is tempted to ask in each case: What am I entitled to infer? Why should I read this study rather than that?

The replacement of consecutive events by static conditions is in keeping with Henri Berr's dictum of 1920: *plus d'histoire événementielle!* Along with people and their actions, another part of history goes into the discard: chronology. Take the work deceptively entitled *France: 1848–1945*, by the well-known Oxford scholar Theodore Zeldin. The two volumes are filled with facts and comments that betoken long and alert research. But the chapters divide social categories, not spans of time: Ambition, Love, Politics, Marriage and Morals, and the like. The author offers his work as a study of the "permanent elements in French society," hoping "to counterbalance the study of events."

To do so he plunges at once into an account of six occupations he thinks characteristic of the bourgeoisie—doctors, notaries, the rich, industrialists, bankers, bureaucrats ("the rich" is apparently an occupation). "How they interacted," we are told, and "how they related to the rest of the country is a complex affair." One would think so, the "they" being difficult to define and to keep from straying. They are presented through selected anecdotes; one has the impression of reading an early chronicle: so-and-so did this; someone else did that. But in chronicles the facts all belong to one year or one month. Here the dates range over the whole ninety-seven years, implying that the categories did not change. Yet readers of "conventional history" are aware that, for example, doctors in 1848 were neither so high-placed socially, nor so well paid, as they were in 1945.

Equally disturbing is the character of the sources. A book on marriage by one Joseph Droz testifies to what was thought *in print* in 1806. Unfortunately, it is quoted from in flatly contradictory ways a few pages apart. Next, a book of 1883 specifies three motives for marriage: convenience, sympathy or love, and duty. But surely convenience and duty are correlative, the girl's duty being the convenience of both families and perhaps the husband's? With another jump in dates we hear that a poll of 1947 overwhelmingly cited love as the preferred reason for marrying. How do we deduce from all this the "permanent elements of French society?" No answer is given; nor can we discern any in the ensuing quotations from the plays of Dumas fils and Henri Bordeaux, the essays of Michelet, and various novels from Flaubert to Proust. Indeed, a quotation from Flaubert is used with its evident irony missed.

My concern here is not so much with the author's method—shaky though it is—as with his purpose. Suppose Mr. Zeldin's aim fully realized, would we have a history? I think not. What then could we call his work? I suggest that the right name is *retrospective sociology*. Why does it not qualify as true social history? Because it disregards chronology and narrative continuity. Social history shows the conditions of life changing in time. But can what I call retrospective sociology not find a place in history? It can. The great third chapter in Macaulay's *History of England* is an attempt to reconstruct the state of society in 1685. That is my point: Macaulay's description bears a date and fits into the narrative; it is the backdrop to the forward movement of namable, datable events. I defy anyone to fit Mr. Zeldin's disjointed, time-free materials into any sequence.

And these materials, as he tells us repeatedly, do not satisfy even his own demands. To his six diagnostic professions he says it is "difficult to attribute influence or cohesion in any simple sense." As for "the ambitions of ordinary men, they are unrecorded and difficult to write about." Of "the emotional relations between married couples" [*sic*] he says they are "even more difficult to trace than what a husband expected from a wife. The answers throughout the period are varied."

Someone might infer from these confessions of futility that a poor example of the genre had been chosen. The reviews say the contrary; they say it is excellent, fresh, instructive history. The same genre using the same method has for a decade earned the highest praise for Fernand Braudel. Only very recently has a critic in the *Times Literary Supplement* ventured to murmur about the nakedness of Braudel's muse—the absence of wars, diplomacy, dynastic change, and other events, all now missing from her professional attire. And as J. H. Plumb noted in Braudel, a characteristic trait of the Annalist *is* futility: "The evidence is slender, uncertain, disparate: the margins of error, Braudel admits, are so very great that the calculations are almost meaningless. And the upshot is [what we already] knew from scores of literary sources."

Even if a fearless type should arise and produce a history for the public—a Prescott or Burckhardt, a Macaulay or John Richard Green, a Michelet or Mommsen—it is doubtful whether the public would greet the book with enthusiasm. Educated general readers have lost certain tastes and acquired others. In fiction, as in history, they no longer care for plot or even narrative. They want states of mind (*mentalités*), strange detail, analytic depth—which is why they relish psychobiography and biography in general, provided it bulges with "revealing details" and hostile opinions of the central figure.

The public, moreover, has picked up somehow, at second hand from the philosophers—or perhaps from *War and Peace* or *The Charterhouse of Parma*—a radical skepticism about historical truth. There has been so much talk about "metahistory," so much theorizing about what the past is, how we know it, and who can possibly reconstruct it, that the intelligent layman is now proud of disbelieving: the record is crooked, the real past irrecoverable. If one protests, the rejoinder comes pat: "Revisionism has shown up one myth after another; history is politically motivated—indeed, history is a weapon in the class struggle; the heroes of old were ordinary men, after all, and they had no influence on events: forces do it all."

From time to time, it is true, the public mind is arrested by some new "interpretation," preferably a diagnosis: the Roman Empire fell owing to gout, or perhaps it was lead poisoning, or both. Now that *is* interesting. The eye brightens at "the bacchanalian appetites of ancient Rome" and the menace of their lead pots. More generally, philosophies of history receive attention for a brief while. Toynbee supplied some good repeatable phrases suggestive of natural laws. But *reading history* is a lost avocation.

Am I not overlooking the vogue of historical fiction? The late Louis L'Amour made a good thing out of it, including a Congressional Medal. In France historical novels sell widely, and the crime-fiction genre is now exploiting the past as a setting for murder and detection. But the best of them do no more than parade quaint detail. Attitude and language are usually modern, anachronistic, and no comparison is remotely possible with Scott, Manzoni, or Dumas.

If the novel is not the place to look for good fictional history, what about film and television? Here again, what attracts is costume—hence Galsworthy's *Forsyte Saga* and other English period pieces from the BBC. Next comes a new genre, the docudrama, which in its patchwork of old newsreels makes the uninformed believe that they are *seeing* history. But enough touted samples of this genre have raised legal and other protests to warrant saying that it is anti-historical in spirit and method. Shakespeare's history plays are models of scholarship compared with the docudramas now produced.

As to film, a critic of the art tried to explain "Why Today's Films Turn to History." Apart from good comments on particular films, he found little more to say than that "the past can be very useful in providing the distance and detachment through which we can discern the pattern of the present." And he quoted Santayana's well-worn tag about those who ignore history having to repeat it. I like that word *distance*, too. In the historical films I have seen, the distance between the screening and the facts was enormous. One wonders, besides, how a smooth-over portrait like *Gandhi* can "reveal the pattern of the present." One is told that in the Polish film about Danton, the hero is "not unlike Lech Walesa," a resemblance certainly not inspired by the historical sense. Again, one is gratified to hear from another reviewer of *Danton* that "compared to the massive scale of the Russian revolution, the French Revolution of 1789 seems almost to have been a chamber piece."

These remarks indicate the *mentalités* of those professionally connected with film when they encounter the historical. One recalls with dismay that M. Ophuls, the maker of the French film about the German occupation of France, has since declared in a book on that film that his so-called documentary is fiction too. In filming it, he says, his feelings toward one or another *actor* would change from day to day and he would alter the emphasis of the film accordingly, wobbling as to who was a villain or a patriot. This unpleasant thought brings back to mind a novelist's description of another film-maker: "He comes as close to historical accuracy as it's possible to come without actually telling the truth."

There is one last corner of society in which history lives or is traditionally expected to live—the schools. Its required study was intended to give it perpetuity through the minds of the young. But history has been given up in thirty states, without causing much outcry. Anyhow, a liking for history has never been common among the young; it is a mature taste that calls for some experience of life. Jane Austen in *Northanger Abbey* has her young heroine, Catherine Morland, say of history: "I read it a little as a duty; but it tells me nothing that does not either vex or weary me. The men are all good for nothing and hardly any women at all." Today, the young are worse than vexed and wearied; they resent, when they do not deny, the reality of the past.

In any case, school history is rarely taught attractively or thoroughly. It seems symptomatic that the excellent Landmark Series of history books for young people has been discontinued for lack of customers. And no wonder. Three years ago, as a consultant to a Commission on History Teaching subsidized by the National Endowment for the Humanities, I visited a number of elementary and high school classes in history in one New England state. The schools were clearly above average and history was given without dilution by "social studies." In both the seventh and the eleventh grades, the make-believe of "research" dominated. The thirteen-year-olds heard the teacher rattle off facts already written on the board about the Stamp Act and its sequel; then the class was loosed on a shelf of paperbacks, in which they were to find additional details to write down—but not in individual notebooks. This was team research, lying or sitting on the floor, one child serving as scribe and plying pencil over a scrap of paper flat on the carpet. The assignment for a history essay to be done at home in a fortnight was: "Describe the character of Thoreau from three points of view—that of his fellow-townspeople in Concord, his own, and that of a soap opera."

In the high-school research, I was invited to assist. The class, the teacher, and I trooped into the library, disturbing the few studious youngsters there, and we pulled out recent issues of the *Reader's Guide*, hoping to find at least two articles about some great figure in a country of our choice. The pair of girls under my wing had chosen, one Egypt, the other Greece. With a little help they found the subject headings, but had difficulty with the next step. In the volume at hand there was one article about Sadat and one about Cleopatra, but not two about either or anybody else. These perplexities of research were to be noted for discussion when we were back in class, and on the way the consensus was that the exercise was one of the less interesting. I should have been there the previous week, when a prepared debate took place among champions of capitalism, socialism, and anarchism. The girl who had chosen Egypt had impersonated Karl Marx and got the winning vote of the class.

In another high school the striking fact was the pairing of history courses in the catalogue. All were elective and the first in each pair sounded solid enough. The second was more enticing: "Men and Women in European History." It was described as "specially designed for those who do not feel equal to the demands of regular history." Since the collapse of the Western Civilization course, the college freshman can usually boast a *tabula rasa* with respect to history.

Between school visits I looked at half a dozen textbooks in American history. All, of course, carefully avoided using so damning a title. They used words like *adventure* or *experiment*, coupled with the name of the country or its adjective. All were quarto size, heavy, and extravagantly illustrated. Double-page spreads in four colors made sure that any threat of consecutive thought had been repelled. The text was a thin stream meandering among maps, portraits, landscapes, statistics neatly boxed, captions, and questions: "How old do you think Benjamin Franklin was when this picture was drawn?" Each text had a teacher's manual full of suggestions from which one could measure the author's automatically low estimate of the teacher's stock of knowledge.

Throughout, the principle seems to be: incoherence—bits and pieces, as in the outside world. Attention must be caught by the picturesque, and kept continually revived by some activity, even if that entails make-believe. When it is not filmstrips or field trips, the game of research is the standby. But even if the pupil can only fumble, is not research the way to learn what historians do?

What they do it for is the unresolved question. We can hardly blame the schools, the textbook writers, least of all the young, when so many habits of mind and clear preferences in modern life work against the writing and the relishing of history. In becoming specialists, historians have helped to breed specialist readers—people who read nothing but, say, Civil War military history or who go in for what is known as industrial archaeology—finding the sites of old foundries all over the county. The histories that sell are for these "buffs." In a book I once opened at random, my eye fell on a sentence that typifies the outlook: "The French Revolution was a disaster for dentistry."

Assuming a readable history, what is the use of reading it? In the most general terms, it is to extend one's experience. Everybody has an individual history—the events that one has shaped into patterns or the tale of last week's shocking incident. History—like happiness—is within you. Reading history adds to this funded experience the experience of one's tribe and of the rest of mankind. It should come to us clarified and memorable.

But has this experience any obvious and immediate use? What need is there to be familiar with what is dead and gone? It is hard enough to be of one's own time; and the best minds today prefer to study the future. It is not sufficiently recognized that our present views of what we want and can reach by living forward are the product of an extensive past. By an habitual awareness of its make-up we can learn to sort out our wishes and perhaps improve the means of controlling our future. Not that studying history imparts formulas and recipes; it develops connoisseurship in human affairs, the intuition of what is likely and what is important.

Ortega judged modern man "emptied of his own history," and he thought contemporary statesmen far less familiar with the relevant past than those of the seventeenth century, when good histories were hard to come by. For all leaders of opinion and action, familiarity with history would seem indispensable, since their chosen lot is to make things work and history tells how things go. It develops foresight and diagnostic skill because it is concrete *and confused*. Studies of the kind I have called retrospective sociology afford no such enhancement of vision, because they focus on single topics. They cut a cross section at right angles to the flow of events, whereas history is the account of the whole tangled mess in all domains simultaneously.

Ideally, the story should show acts and thoughts intertwined as they occur—politics, art, business, religion, fashion, sport, folly, and crime. But a story needs a pattern that can be grasped and retained. "History is what you can remember." So historians have traditionally divided total history into a few broad kinds. In each kind some aspect predominates—politics, economics, culture. The other doings of the population are there, too, in the background or middle ground. But in any kind of history, only the facts of political life can provide the framework, the skeleton, because politics is the most continuous and most striking human activity; it affects the whole society; and it is the most readily understood. It may take years of study for a reader in the western world to comprehend the religions of the Far East, but it takes him no time at all to imagine a palace revolution in China, India, or Japan.

To save history from the encroachment of radically different inquiries implies no disparagement of generalities in the social studies or any other department of thought. A hundred years ago, a description of what history is and does would have been unnecessary; the nineteenth century was addicted to reading history; it was an accepted mode of thought, as one may see in Shaw's prefaces to his plays and even in his letters. But theory, generality, abstraction have by now displaced the concrete imagination of past events. Material "fragments of history," as the newspapers call them, are no substitute, and this deficiency works to our disadvantage.

On this point, the remarks of the Israeli diplomat Abba Eban are decisive. Discussing current trends in training for international affairs, Dr. Eban said: "I don't really think it can compare with the vivid, living spectacle of history. And if one had to sacrifice something, I would prefer to sacrifice the somewhat abstract jargon of these analyses, rather than the direct contemplation of the predicaments in which nations have found themselves."

The nineteenth century took to history not for the good of the state, but for pleasure. We need to be reminded of this fact just as, in our study-ridden culture, we need to be reminded that works of art are for pleasure too. The pleasures of reading history are manifold: it exercises the imagination and furnishes it, discloses the nuances of the familiar within the unfamiliar, brings out the heroic in mankind side by side with the vile, tempers absolute partisanship by showing how few monsters of error there have been, and in all these ways induces a relative serenity. This composure is not to be taken for cynical indifference. Rather, it is a state of spirited pessimism like that generated by reading the great novels and epics.

Candor compels the student of history to deal with the skepticism that exists about his field, as well as the more recent complaint that reading American and European history today is provincial and futile. We ought, instead, to learn all about Africa and the Far East, with which our relations are "crucial." This objection has already led to changes in school and college programs; one has even heard of high schools that "foster world understanding" by having the Home Economics department teach pupils how to prepare "an Oriental meal." This nonsense can only foster a vast misunderstanding. The Far East does not consist of a handful of nations very much alike; it is a huge congeries of peoples with traditions as different from one another as those of the many European or American nations. India alone, with its three hundred languages and diverse religious and ethnic hostilities, requires years of study before one can be said to understand it. Africa presents the same difficulties—to which one must add, for all these regions, the need to master languages extremely "foreign" and complex. Supposing all these conditions met, the reader who had at length acquired a good grasp of those histories would, if he lacked knowledge of his own Western tradition, still be far from a world outlook.

A more reasonable objection to seeking historical knowledge is the philosophical doubt about the nature of history itself: how can it be true? Historians disagree and keep rewriting their accounts of the same events. Revisionism never ends. As for the classic historians—are they not all wrong, being out of date? And even worse, do they not deal solely with battles and kings, instead of telling how the people lived? Apparently, a democratic age, if it is to pay attention to the past, must be given one that corresponds to its present preoccupations.

With this last demand the wheel has come full circle: we are back in the hands of the retrospective sociologists who want to help solve current problems by looking at likely precedents. Everybody is of course free to prefer such works to history, but social studies will never impart a comprehensive sense of the past nor stir the historical imagination. Nor should the cant about battles and kings and the absence of "the people" in narrative histories be believed. All the great histories describe the common ways of life and thought, and if they name the shakers and movers who made the conspicuous events happen, it is because their omission would be to eliminate the *story* from history.

What of the charge of uncertain truth? Why is history rewritten every twenty years; why do no two histories say exactly the same thing on the same topic? Because the subject of history is life, and its elements and their relations are not exhausted by any recital. Every historian makes his own pattern out of what he finds in the record; he reconstructs actuality by means of his controlled imagination. Barring provable mistakes, which others soon point out, his story is as true as any other that is likewise conscientious. All are incomplete, and as the passage of time breeds new concerns and new conceptions, the past appears under new lights. The reader of history accordingly reads two, three, five, ten accounts of the same period, and though he finds a variety of meanings propounded, he also finds a large body of identical fact. Whoever wants the total reality must first gain access to the mind of God.

As to obsolescence, the modern editions of the classic historians correct the errors in footnotes, and it is remarkable how little difference these changes make. The most important modify a portrait: somebody was or was not responsible for a certain action, or had a motive higher or lower than the one originally assigned. Such corrections usually come from a painstaking biographer, which raises the question, Why does not biography confer all the benefits of history, and more agreeably at that? The answer is that in biography, scale and proportions are skewed by putting the single life at the center of the world for three hundred pages. Emerson was wrong to say that history is but a collection of biographies, for if these "lives" are well composed each is a complete pattern and they cannot be added together.

Finally, it must be understood that "reading history" does not mean "covering" any particular region or period. To be sure, the wider the scope, the stronger the power of judgment becomes and the greater the sympathy and regard for what humanity has achieved in the teeth of its own defects. History is indeed what Gibbon said it was—a long tale of crimes and follies. But it is more than that; it is also the story of genius and daring and dumb, oxlike persistence—virtues without which mankind would not have got as far as discovering that living in caves was a good idea. Not just to know but to feel these truths is to confirm Burckhardt's dictum about the value of cultivating history: "not to be cleverer the next time, but wiser forever."

What Critics
Are Good For

The artist's rejoinder to the question implied in the title above is absolute and consistent through the ages: critics are good for nothing. Swift long ago summed up the artist's case: "critics are the drones of the learned world, who devour the honey, and will not work themselves." Other great artists have filled out the indictment: critics are ignorant; they corrupt public taste, attack and destroy genius; they are failed artists or they would not be critics; they belong (said Swift again) with the whores and the politicians. The only writer I have come across who had a good word for critics was Josh Billings. He was a humorist and may have been ironic: "To be a good critic," he said, "demands more brains and judgment than most men possess." A modest claim, but it leaves untouched the artist's grievance: What need for critics at all?

The answer would seem self-evident. Art does not disseminate itself unaided. Artists need heralds, go-betweens, not to say procurers. The worst environment for an artist in a high civilization is dead silence.

To keep art from being stillborn is a worthy role. When Plato said of Socrates' mother, "Midwives are respectable women and have a character to lose," he was alluding to Socrates' notion of himself as midwife to ideas. For the same reason, critics are to be respected—and attacked. Artist and critic are like the sexes at war, capital and labor, author and publisher—opposing forces which out of conflict engender.

Reviewers, the most potent of critics, are understandably the most abused. The young Goethe cried: "Kill the dog, he's a reviewer." That is a tenable policy, but to ask critics to be creators before they can criticize is foolish. One does not need to be a cook in order to say that there is too much salt in the omelet. And some reviewers, harassed as they are by the daily grind of reporting on mediocre work, are candid about their shortcomings. One English drama critic, who wrote part of his column before seeing the play, confessed: "My two million readers have to know about it, whether I do or not."

As for the artist's wish to be judged only by other artists, it is not a Utopian dream but sheer folly. Artists are notoriously blind to any kind of work but their own, although when not jealous or narrow-sighted they may be excellent judges of technique and purport. Perceptive or not, they play a part in the making of fame— or obstruct it. Flaubert, for example, read Stendhal's *The Red and the Black* twenty years after its appearance and long before it was admired. He says: "I find it badly written and incomprehensible as to intention and characters. I have never understood what Balzac saw in him." In his own day, Stendhal got a similar verdict from his friend and fellow novelist Mérimée: "Why did you choose a hero who is surely impossible, and why, having chosen him, did you bedizen him with traits of your own invention? Not one of his actions do I find in keeping with his character."

Either of these judgments would damn a reviewer for all time. And speaking of time, what artists would consent to waste theirs by writing about each other's works? When forced to do so by financial need, artists like Shaw and Berlioz resented the slavery, and the world regrets the works lost by such journeyman tasks.

The conclusion is inescapable: criticism must be left in the hands of those who want to do it. Critics must be on hand to give access to art, and just as there are many genres and many sorts of difficulty in past and present art, so there must be different types of critic— from the textual to the impressionist and from the formal to the cultural. Of course, in addition to these differences, the critic's intelligence, education, and above all, sensory acuteness and moral make-up determine his fitness to deal with a work or type of work. Much bad criticism is due to a mismatch between artist and critic on the plane of temperament and sensibility.

Criticism itself is not one thing. Its scope and character have changed over time as its powers and vocabulary have developed; nothing about it was ready-made from the start. In Dante's sequence of poems called *La Vita Nuova*, one finds appended to many of them a prose commentary. It tells the reader what is said in the first four lines of the poem and the next six, and so on. Dante evidently felt that his contemporaries needed that sort of help, in addition to a few moral and theological explanations.

The Renaissance critics, armed with the Greek and Roman classics, felt it their duty to assess modern work by rules derived, legitimately or not, from the ancients. The critic became a judge who questions the culprit and condemns or acquits him according to law. Since the decline of that neoclassic idea, critics have abandoned this absolutism and become historical and relativist. They describe the setting of the work, explain its form, list or palliate faults, and declare success or failure. Critics of this stripe are out to change our minds.

Their opponents, the formalists, believe that works of art are "autonomous creations obeying laws of their own" and are best considered as having no relation to life. Thus, no reference to history, biography, or influence is licit. Such critics are barely willing to explain the changed meanings of words, which is of course a piece of history. They prefer to talk about structure, metaphor, rhetoric, images, themes, and myths. In the fine arts, they interpret symbols (another bit of history), and more abstractly discuss space, perspective, diagonals, triangles, the golden section, color theory, and what they insist on calling rhythm. Similarly in music and theatre, each kind of critic finds his chosen elements and considers them sufficient to "give access." But whereas the historical critic is ready to concede value to the formalist, the latter excommunicates his rival.

The plasticity of great art, its hospitality to new interpretations, makes of the critic a permanent institution. He may find a new work in an old text, that is to say, he redirects our attention to revive appreciation, rescue from neglect, and rehabilitate the condemned. The notion of an all-wise Posterity settling merit forever is a myth. But the later comers that make up posterity have this advantage, that they come to *some* works equipped with the judgments, catchwords, and clichés uttered before their time—by critics, echoed in the schoolbooks. The prime example of both the failure and the function of Posterity is found in the history of Shakespeare's reputation. The transformation of his figure from a wild barbaric songster into a great artist was the work of an intense concentration of critics.

For such a change to occur, there must be enough new opinion to silence the old. It is a mistake to think that about any artist or work of art there is ever a consensus. Dislike, indifference, misunderstanding continue. Excellent judges remain unmoved by the approval of the supposed majority, but their dissent stays quiet—a concealed anarchy. Dominant and subdued judgments coexist, and the balance is ever precarious, because the world and its moods change and bring on different desires and demands.

Sixty years ago, as I can testify, Mozart was deemed a frivolous, superficial entertainer, not to be mentioned in the same breath with Beethoven and Wagner. A liking for Italian opera was the mark of the musical vulgarian. At that time also, Dickens was accounted a crude and sentimental novelist who had written for housemaids; now that housemaids were gone forever, he would be unread and disappear. Nor did Henry James fare any better. Nobody could call him crude; his designation was: "social twitterer," fussing over inessentials in tortuous sentences. As for the baroque in painting, sculpture, and architecture, it was nothing but childish extravagance. Bernini? A pandering profiteer. Rubens? An interior decorator.

Sometimes the return to favor of an artist or a period comes about at the behest of a single voice—if the time is ripe and if the voice has authority. After T. S. Eliot had certified that Kipling was a poet, it was no longer permissible to despise him as a journalist whose day had passed. The literati cowed by Eliot very likely did not go back to reading Kipling with fervor, but another rehabilitation did attract a new public. This return to favor was achieved by Harold Nicolson in behalf of Tennyson. By 1920, Tennyson had lost his immense fame as a poet. He was one of the Victorians, and Lytton Strachey had just shown what frauds they all were. Nicolson argued his case on the principle that ethical poetry antedates Victorianism and forms the bulk of all poetry ever written. A poet, moreover, must be judged by his best work, not his worst. The argument proved convincing, and in due course T. S. Eliot turned his solemn gaze on Tennyson and nodded approval. Tennyson was back in the pantheon.

What is worth noting about this particular case is that forty years later, in a second edition of Nicolson's book, the poor author had to defend himself against the charge of "cruel bias" against Tennyson. The generation of the sixties had found in Tennyson "spiritual unrest" and other endearing traits, such as his father's alcoholism, and these Nicolson had not valued properly. So the critic who single-handed had rehabilitated the poet was now counted among his detractors. Who says that critics have things all their own way?

Tennyson's case reminds us that in the past one of the duties of criticism was to report whether the tendency of a work was moral or immoral. The practice was no Victorian innovation; it was taken for granted by the ancients, the Renaissance, and the neoclassic writers. Dr. Johnson was as much a moralist critic as Dr. Bowdler, though they would have differed in their particular decisions. Today, as everybody knows, a concern with morality in art is considered quaint, not to say absurd and philistine.

On reflection, moral judgment in the arts appears rather as a tribute to their power to influence emotion and possibly conduct. And reflecting further on what some critics do today, one sees that a good many have merely shifted the ground of their moralism, transferring their impulse of righteousness to politics and social issues. Not long ago a critic discussing the legacy of Matthew Arnold called it with disapproval "an agency of the capitalist hegemony." Contemporary poets and playwrights are classified as revolutionary, reactionary, elitist, or populist with the same old moral animus. And still other critics praise or blame according to religious, ethnic, or sexual criteria.

These attributions match the artists' own biases. Modernism appears to require a hostility to existing institutions that amounts to a a political creed, just as the sympathy with the masses, the poor, the oppressed, and the colloquial is a moral or religious position. That being so, if a critic comes to his subject with a belief or a bias it may be of service to art in the perennial battle of ideas, in the unavoidable diversity of ethical and intellectual convictions. Critics are needed to defend one side and the other against cultural totalitarianism.

Since artists and critics are a feature of our unexampled pluralism, the notion of an ideal critic, one who is not only certified perfectly balanced mentally, but also capable of judging art exclusively as art, is a mistaken ideal. It springs from that other mistaken notion, the autonomy of art, and its twin belief in something called the aesthetic experience. This last term is at best a prideful synonym for the alert perception of art; for what is felt and perceived in art is not really separable from preexisting mental and emotional attachments. The intake does not cause a distilled state of mind cut off from the rest. As the pleasures art affords differ from the sensual while relying on the senses, they likewise partake of all other pleasures—intellectual, affectional, and spiritual. In short, the phrase "pure art" does not correspond to any reality.

If the critic's role is truly defined by these concerns and these services to art and the public, then critics have a right to live, even when stupid or biased. But their justification vanishes if they abandon *maieutics*—midwifery. The current style of writing about the arts not only fails to perform the due "delivery" of art to the mind but also obstructs the process by which it might occur. Here are some instances of the malpractice:

- "In the final scene the plot finally assumes its status as the crown of an intricate development of poetic resources."
- "Control of the subject, coupled with irony, gives astringency to both foreground and background of the emotion."
- "The formal interplay of colors and shapes creates forces of both harmony and tension . . . while the linear design composed of all the edges of tone and color-masses weave [*sic*] a unifying rhythmic network throughout the painting."
- "[The hero's] consciousness grows larger than life, or than death, to show that life itself is large and cannot be detached in the reclusive self, framed in the indefectibility of the portrait, which no longer attests to life, hung up in the closed consciousness."

These examples come from reputable sources—a newspaper, a college text, an encyclopedia, a literary journal. Clearly, Critics' English is no longer explanatory. The use of words in a figurative sense does not let up. To read criticism nowadays is to slog through sentences full of *tension, rhythm, control; structure, texture, dynamics; restraint, irony, lyricism; icon, epiphany, dimension, distancing, metaphor*—above all, metaphor—and hardly any of these used in either a literal or technical sense.

As a result, the language of criticism sounds identical with the prose of the advertiser of fashions: vague images create the illusion of moving among luxurious things. The word *metaphor* itself typifies the vacancy of mind. It has been so debased as to qualify even what does not exist. Thus in a review of a singer whose upper register had faded we read: "She turned this to her advantage, using it as a metaphor for the uneasy yearnings of the Mahler songs."

Now, metaphor implies a comparison among four terms. If one says "the ship plows the sea," the meaning is that just as the plow in its forward motion divides the soil, so the ship moves and divides the sea. Without four terms, no metaphor. Hence there is no discoverable meaning in praising a sculptor for "his way with three-dimensional metaphors" or in saying that in literature the mention of food "serves up many metaphors." We may wonder why critics, who are certainly educated people of uncommon ability, have adopted this reverse English, which destroys integrity and beauty at one stroke. They cannot all be simply perverse. Rather, they have succumbed to certain widespread social attitudes. They have, on the one hand, aped what everybody now does with language, and, on the other, they have yielded to what everybody thinks criticism is.

In both tendencies one detects the cult of creativity. Do something new, original, startling; above all, be yourself and therefore disregard common rules, feel free to violate usage, show off your imagination and your specialty. From this cluster of precepts come the new words and phrases that gain currency in business, government, and the professions. Sad to say, business and criticism and the formerly "plain man" share the compulsion to dress up what is felt as a too commonplace reality. In short, everybody wants to be a poet, not knowing that real poets do not dress up reality but transfix it.

How and when did this aberration come about? Toward the end of the nineteenth century, with the rapid expansion of schooling, of the reading public, of production in the arts, a sense that confusion was growing at the same pace overcame the intellectual world. The need for order magnified the critic's role, and the "creative critic" was invented. Oscar Wilde was his strongest proponent. Conscious of great powers, he established the dogma that to criticize justly called for genius of as high an order as that needed to make the object being criticized. The greater subtlety and complexity of modern art, which required of the beholder acute perceptiveness and special information, seemed to justify the claim. Only a critic who was an artist to his fingertips could train the beholder's faculties. Henry James, who had latterly suffered much from critics, nonetheless begged for "the beneficent play of criticism," pointing out that it was "the only gate of appreciation, just as appreciation is, in regard to a work of art, the only gate of enjoyment." And he deplored the "huge array of producers and readers" who flounder in "production uncontrolled, production untouched by criticism, unguided, unlighted, uninstructed, unashamed, on a scale that is really a new thing in the world."

The creative critic took up his new duties by sitting neither at the feet of the artist as interpreter, nor above him as judge of performance, but side by side with him as partner reenacting the feat of creation. Criticism thus expanded into aesthetics, the forerunner of the current rarefied modes of writing about art—poetical, psychological, or metaphysical. The critic, in this situation, sees a double chance. He naturally identifies himself with the artist and he soon thinks he is one; and because his task is analytic, he readily begins to talk like a scientist. As we saw, his favorite words have the aura of technicality. Control, tension, negative space are laboratory words. And most critics being now academics as well, they must have system and method.

In this transformation, the critic's natural audience and his raison d'être alike have disappeared. The reader finds only puzzlement as the critic applies his method, conducts his "analysis," no longer to "open the gate of appreciation" (by now a bad word), but to demonstrate that the work of art under the microscope is an object entirely different from what it seems to the naked eye. This treatment of art naturally goes with giving up the idea that art should be enjoyed: it is too important for pleasure; it is meant to be studied, which in turn enables us to admire the analyst. In sum, the critic's role as giver of access to art has been negated, and Henry James's hope of production guided by critics, defeated.

Having given the earlier, midwife critic what history shows to be his due, I must now appear to take it back by adding the caveat uttered long ago by the American critic John Jay Chapman: "Criticism is powerless to reach art, because art exists in a region beyond the reach of other expression." In a word, "we cannot hope to know what art is." These sentiments seem to rule out the utility of critics. How can the contradiction be resolved? In the usual way, by a distinction that should be of concern to critics and artists alike. Chapman was being a good critic when he warned his reader against believing that words about art explain the essence or fix the locus of the thing itself. Chapman's contemporary William James, himself an artist in words and paint, made the same observation when reviewing his student Berenson's book on the Florentine painters: "The difference between the first and second-best things in art absolutely seems to escape verbal definition—it is a matter of a hair, a shade, an inward quiver of some kind—yet what miles away in point of preciousness!"

Where do these disclaimers leave the critic? If he cannot touch the spot where art resides, what is he so busy doing? To answer is but to restate that the critic clears the path *to* the work and *through* the work by removing inner and outer causes of confusion. If he could do more and tell the secret of creation, the making of great art would be open to all, a matter of formula.

These sobering thoughts bring on the final question: What is art, then, that we can't know what it is? Granting with Chapman that we cannot define or seize the essence, we can perhaps define the enterprise—not what art is, but what it does. A traditional answer is that art imitates life. This has been refined into other propositions: art *mirrors* life; art *re-creates* life; art *expresses* the artist's *intuition of life*, or his *criticism of life*. The modern view, as we know, is that artists fashion autonomous structures into which we read whatever our experience or fantasies suggest.

There is truth in each of these propositions; and also room for error. I prefer to say that art is an extension of life. Art uses the physical materials of ordinary experience—words, pigment, sound, wood, stone or anything else—and puts them together in such a way that the sensations they set off arouse our memories of living, add to them, and thereby extend our life. Idiom ought to permit: "I spent part of last year in Rubens; I have lived the Berlioz *Requiem*, I often travel to *Middlemarch*."

Annexing these portions of art-made experience, undergoing this stirring up of what we have felt, serves to clarify existence, complexify it, and sometimes falsify it. In any of its roles, art casts an intense light on the great questions and events—birth, death, love, fame, the body and the soul.

If this is true, we can understand why criticism cannot capture the being and ultimate meaning of art, why there can be no consensus about art, artists, and works of art. For no agreement is conceivable about Being and the ultimate meaning of life. Art and life are kindred kaleidoscopes, shifting even as we look at them; they do not impose a uniform pattern on all minds but may be "taken" in a myriad ways. In re-forming our view of experience through order and clarity, art brings out novelties and ambiguities no one suspected: it is a second life and an extraordinary one. That common words, and patches of oil on canvas, and vibrating strings are able to do this is a mystery, and though we "cannot hope to know what art is," we know that it somehow captures and holds up to our gaze the mystery of existence.

Reckoning with Time and Place

Being a student of history and formerly engaged in the strange ritual of teaching it (strange, because, properly, it can only be read), I have had numberless times in my mind and on my lips the phrase "sense of the past." As I look back and look within, seeking ways to make a little clearer this notion of a special sense distinct from the contents of memory, I find that the phrase itself is, for me, associated with some few uses of it and statements about it. I tend to think first of Henry James's unfinished novel (but completed plot), which has the phrase for a title and which goes at great length into the quirks and shocks caused by the divided feeling of Then and Now. At times, the thought of James brings up the play *Berkeley Square*, based on the novel and made acceptable to the late 1930s by the fine acting of Leslie Howard, who was shortly to perish in the Atlantic while flying on a wartime mission to Lisbon. Here memory suddenly joins to fact, a feeling of "how strangely remote the atmosphere of these clustered thoughts, yet how fully understood," which I take to be the emotion, the coloring of the sense of the past.

From this double awareness I jump to Lionel Trilling's essay, titled like the novel, but devoted to a different use of the phrase. It was written and published in 1942, the very year (or perhaps the one before?) when Howard died—or was it? I must look it up, if I am to relive the time with confidence. Trilling's essay is linked with the thought of the play, because his subject is literature first and history second. His purpose was to show the error of those who declared art and literature totally disjunct. The New Criticism had

75

by then conquered the leading minds concerned with high culture, and any critic with historical ideas in his head was ipso facto a laggard if not a philistine. "The poem itself," the painting as an arrangement of lines, planes, and colors free of meaning or emotion; "absolute music"—those were the axioms, after having been for several decades the slogans.

Not only critics but connoisseurs also were now bound to abide by these exclusionary rules, or at least to talk the language of autonomy and purity. For the first time, the public became aware that there was a *theory* of literature, which bound together and guaranteed fixed truths about art. The familiar spectacle of clashing or superseding tastes and fashions, doctrines and schools, was implicitly denied; it belonged to history and, as in another famous theory in the neighboring realm of social revolution, the chaos of history was to come to an end.

The curious and paradoxical features of this onslaught on "historical criticism," so-called, is that it professed to defend art against "science." The New Critics' attack would have been justified if it had confined itself to making it clear that the scholars who talked history and biography while pretending to discuss poems and novels were mostly dull men, who cared little for literature, whose sense of relevance was weak, and who lacked knowledge or intuition of how artists work. But apart from a broad denunciation of academics, the New Critics "revolted," in Trilling's words, "against the scientific notion of the fact as transferred in a literal way to the study of literature." This singular belief that history is a form of science can only be accounted for by the assumption that facts exist only for scientists and that the apparatus of verification is the sign of this monopoly.

Against this gravamen Trilling's essay defended the proposition that historical and biographical elements were so closely interwoven with the substance of art—indeed, are so often part of what is felt and relished in the encounter with art—that representing those facts as an alien intrusion was untenable: "In certain cultures the pastness of a work of art gives it an extra-aesthetic authority which is incorporated into its aesthetic power. But even in our own culture with its ambivalent feeling about tradition, there inheres in a work of art of the past a certain quality, an element of its aesthetic existence, which we can identify as its pastness . . . side by side with the formal elements. . . ."

The excuse that may be offered for the New Critics' misconception of history is that in the late nineteenth century, when the academics who later taught literature were in their formative years, some historians did put forward the claim that their work was scientific. They were defending their domain against the aggressive self-conceit of the newly redefined "social sciences" and boasting to the world of their own "method" and "rigor." They repudiated those who wrote "literary" history and they eagerly gave up panoramic narratives for narrow "studies," microscopic in detail and free of ideas. In their place, "problems" became the sole justification of research. All the difficulties of life had turned into problems, from which it followed that the only worthy effort was to reach solutions. And nothing but science had solved or would ever solve a problem.

The paradox in the New Critics' assault is that under its pressure departments of English in colleges and universities began to admit avowed critics into their ranks; and as soon as this surrender occurred, the New Criticism became a method; the study of literature was turned into problem-solving, while the creation of the work was also regarded as a problem that the author had or had not successfully solved. The metaphors had to "work out," the structure to be tested at every joint; nothing flawed or excrescent could pass this engineering survey.

Of course the theory could not stand still. It had to be revised as fresh material underwent examination. And thus the procession of system after system in criticism got under way. The New Critics with their "close reading" borrowed from French *explication de texte* were soon joined by quantifiers emulating the ways long used in Shakespeare scholarship, and the hunt began for myths, themes, and symbols. These, as the operative parts of the work, must be brought into consciousness if the meaning was to be understood. Regardless of the thing sought, "scrutiny" was the order of the day, as the name of a potent periodical made clear.

Reinforced by the new interest in the metaphysical poets and the revived attention to Dante and Melville, the scrutinizing shortly transformed criticism into the decoding of ciphers. Every piece worth studying was found to contain "levels" of meanings; words and images meant anything but what they seemed to say. In short, the great writers of the world seemed to have worked in one genre only: allegory.

These developments could have been predicted in their general outlines, for the academic world inevitably academicizes whatever it takes up. How else could a collective enterprise such as education and certification require and measure perceptiveness or sensibility? The contempt for "Impressionist Criticism" (that is, for the work of the great critics from Plato and Longinus to Hazlitt and Anatole France) rests on the ground that by definition it is suggestive and not apodictic. Canons and terminology, on the contrary, stimulate ingenuity and foster disputation, which together give a pleasant sense of mastery and comradeship, whereas original intuition is solitary and unsure. Besides, the graduate student who will later teach must also be given a scheme that average intelligence finds manageable.

Thus the arrangement suits everybody: the young faculty member must publish for promotion, and a paper on a problem is the indicated means. There are fourteen previous interpretations of Blake's "Tyger." They all fail, naturally, to prove what the poem means. So with conventional modesty a stronger hypothesis is advanced in the proper journal, first reviewing all the others, to add suitable bulk to the piece. In this manner, assistant professors the world over can count on infinite opportunities to make their mark by adding each a new solution of whatever -tic or -tist species the whirligig of time may bring into fashion.

When art and science become confused by being made alike exercises of the geometrical spirit, the only countervailing form of thought is the historical. History and its temper, the sense of the past, is the exact opposite of the analytic mode: it is intuitive, attached to the particular and the concrete, and respectful of time, where analysis is abstract and methodic, aims at the general, and says that reference to "time when" has nothing to do with the case. One might add that only under this persuasion can criticism boast of being creative; for with the extraction of "images," the use of "models," the reduction to "structure," it has invented something that it can play with unhindered by a feeling for artistic detail—or by the sense of life and likelihood. Method conquers all, and for want of it past ages must have been lost amid the baffling manifestations of literature, music, and paint.

Instead of these riches of analytic thought, the great critics had only insights, glimpses of the truth. "Imitation" and a few maxims constituted their whole stock in trade. They believed, like Molière, that comedy was to amuse by neatly resembling situations in life and making fun of foolish traits, whereby it might cause some moral reflections—*castigat ridendo mores*. They did not suspect that, as in Shakespeare's comedies, it was the language itself that determined the plot and the moral; or that in the best comedies the actions and speeches conform to what we now know about the workings of the unconscious. In the criticism of music, such brilliant performers as E. T. A. Hoffmann and Berlioz did not even suspect the possibilities opened up by Schenker analysis; and when Diderot or Gautier wrote about painting, it was without the solid support of iconography. In a word, lacking the taxonomy, anatomy, physiology, and pathology of art, earlier generations could hardly know what they were beholding, and their talk about what they thought they admired was but an irresponsible wandering among masterpieces.

A few artists in the past did allow philosophical systems to influence their work. Today, the love of system has been more pervasive, and more than one modern artist has composed works with the conscious design of supplying symbols and building layers of meaning suitable for interpretation. It is a notable instance of art imitating not nature but the critics.

All the while it remained true, as Trilling's essay made clear, that no criticism can be written without bringing in matter "extraneous" to the work and without that matter belonging to "history." "The leap of imagination," said Trilling, "which an audience makes when it responds to *Hamlet* is enormous, and it requires a comprehensive, although not necessarily instructed, sense of the past." A child at school reading the play could testify to this truth; he would find some of Shakespeare's wordings strange. And if not instructed in changed meanings, the closest of close readers will misunderstand; he will think that the "conscience" that makes "cowards of us all" is the moral conscience, whereas it is only consciousness, reflection on our present state. But to explain changed meanings is to be an historical critic. No one could know the old usage if no one dabbled in history.

This is reason enough for declining to abolish criticism, yet one may still ask why literature, and contemporary literature in particular, have to be *studied*. It was not till after the middle of the nineteenth century that the arts and letters of modern times entered the curriculum. Earlier, they did not constitute subjects; there were no courses entitled "Spencer, Milton, and Wordsworth." The great novels were read for fun. The shocking innovators of the day—Swinburne or Zola—were read in secret by the young, who also went to see the Impressionists, hear Debussy, and sneak into a private performance of Ibsen.

The causes that brought about the studying of such things, that is, propelled the arts into the academy, are complex and disparate. Cultural nationalism and the nineteenth-century love of history had something to do with it. Shakespeare scholarship offered a precedent, and the suicide of the classical curriculum through pure philology dealt the final blow. "Modern greats" were needed to replace the ancients, deemed useless and out of date by the apostles of practical and "progressive" subjects.

By the 1890s also, the new social sciences (and the "new history" tagging along) scorned the notions derivable from ancient texts, even though it was the old classical scholarship that had established the forms adopted by the new disciplines, and it was history-writing that had transformed the Western tradition into a professional preserve. A sudden enlargement of "the past" took place in the nineteenth century when it "discovered" history, that is, history as important and interesting from beginning to end. For Voltaire, only four ages mattered in the whole sweep from remotest times—the brief high moments of civilization that had produced great art. For Herder, Walter Scott, Michelet, and their fellow Romanticists, every age, every place, every class of people mattered: all had done their part in creating the present.

To that generation, the past was now immense, highly colored, largely unknown; and all of it being formative, it invited study in minutest detail. Every institution, every work of the mind, every surviving object had its history, to be disentangled from the rest if it was to be rightly placed and valued. Things might be puzzling, might seem contrary to reason, but their genesis was the clue. The historical-biographical (and sometimes evolutionary) study of the arts was thus launched as part of the intellectual expansion of Europe in the 1800s; it paralleled its political and social expansion through liberalism and democracy.

This movement ran its course in eighty years, engendering subdivisions and specialisms that turned against their progenitor. When the New Critics denounced historical criticism in the 1920s, they were but one of the groups engaged in a general repudiation of Romanticism. The "failure of Romanticism" had been proclaimed in France in the latter third of the past century and it became, by the first decade of the present one, the dominant politico-cultural view in most of Europe. It reached the United States through numerous channels, one of which has been overlooked and would repay study. I mean the adaptation by Irving Babbitt, professor of French at Harvard, of the arguments deployed by a scholarly baron named Ernest Seillière in a series of volumes that appeared in the decade before the First World War. In them, as in Babbitt and also in the New Critics, Romanticism and Democracy are discredited—the former has failed, the latter has debased culture. As a student of Babbitt's, T. S. Eliot acquired these principles, adopted these sentiments, and in his influential essays translated the French dogmas for English-speaking readers.

In effect, by the 1920s no overt attack on the historical outlook was actually needed. The Romantic century was no longer tolerable, and to destroy it, to pull apart its synthesis, it was enough to declare its elements fallacious and ill-matched, and not to be justified by history. For in using history, one must practice relativism: history relates one thing to another and often suggests an unwelcome dependence and a persistent doubt. The new mood sought an absolutism implying certainty.

But if the grievance is that the historical critics obscure the work by piling up irrelevancies around it, what of the succeeding schools? Have they not wound up in abstruse speculations distant from the work itself? One must then ask, what ground is there for criticism to occupy? In his essay, Lionel Trilling uses for the first time in print the term *cultural criticism*. It implies that the other ground is culture as a whole. The phrase was not invented on purpose to launch a new ism; it arose spontaneously at some unremembered point, after Trilling and I had begun, in the mid-1940s, to teach together at Columbia a seminar that continued to be offered for some twenty-five years.

The seminar was intended to prepare students for the writing of the Ph.D. dissertation. When the applicants for the restricted number of places came to inquire about the work, we would explain it by saying it amounted to cultural criticism: the group would read the books assigned and discuss them with the aid of all relevant knowledge—historical, aesthetic, logical, comparative, philosophical, and all the other adjectives on the literary genres cited in *Hamlet*: no holds barred. But what was relevant? Ah, that was the purpose of the exercise: to develop judgment to the point where nothing foolish, nothing forced, nothing "viewy," nothing unnecessary is used that might stand in the way of understanding and enjoyment. To test the performance, a paper of chapter length was to be written on a subject outside the list of readings.

This joint enterprise, unlikely in the abstract, was possible in fact, because the clarity and openness of the historical outlook gave individual judgment free play. This latitude is the opposite of the desire behind the so-called rigorous methods, which is to coerce—the wish for universal agreement based on methodical proof. To this wish is added the emotional spur that, with luck and hard work, MY theorem or solution will be right and yours wrong. Thanks to the spirit of cultural criticism, Trilling and I were left free, not only from the pressure of each other's predilections, but from that of a doctrine made public, official, and compulsory. As is well known, Trilling's views of the meaning and bearing of art and literature evolved with the passage of time; his judgment of their relation to life became more complex and subtly detailed. But he never had to recant and declare a new critical faith; the views he was still refining and rewording to his very last essay on criticism never contradicted those of the first, never implied a repudiation of the way we had chosen for instructing students of culture or of the role we attributed to the past, and the sense of the past, in cultural creation itself.

Trilling's own critical writings exhibit the fine flower of our joint teaching: historical and "formal" (to use a single word for all the other aspects) in unprescribed proportions, rooted in particulars, and using the imagination to relive the chief impressions that the work may have given in its time or could give in ours. With such criteria in mind, the student papers were read and exhaustively criticized by each of us for sense and form, diction and judgment, sensibility and persuasive force. It never occurred to either of us to codify our non-method—to write a textbook on the practice of cultural criticism, much less to argue its theory against the others, garrisoned in English departments or proliferating on French soil.

For cultural criticism presupposes the factitiousness of theory and the unsuitability of system when it comes to understanding art. One reads a poem as one reads a face—with a great deal of attention, knowledge, and experience of reading. There is only this difference, that one may stare at a poem. As for knowledge and experience, they can grow in regions apparently far from poems. Unexpectedly, long after, a fact or memory links itself with a verse or a rhythm to enrich a true reading. The great point is that none of the elements brought to bear is ever regarded as determinant, as a cause; it is only a condition, whose force is gauged, like everything in immediate experience, by the *esprit de finesse*.

All this imples—indeed, defines—the historical sense, for it is that sixth sense, as Nietzsche rightly took it to be, which quickly divines conditions and their order of rank. Modern philosophies of science have themselves come to call "historical" whatever falls outside their domain of definition and measurability. Their name for this latter realm is not so happily chosen: they call it "lawful," insinuating the idea (without meaning to) that the undefined and unmeasured is anarchy. But of course life, now equated with history, is not anarchical for being regular and irregular, certain and uncertain. It should be called contingent, for it is full of regularities, but no system. That is why the art of living consists in knowing how to discern conditions and weigh the probabilities of their unfolding. It is also why the criticism of art, which is an extension of life, must similarly be of a lifelike complexity.

If this explanation of "cultural criticism" were impugned as being a theory like the rest—"for doesn't every activity imply a theory?"—the answer would be obvious: theory if you like, but of a disarming simplicity—no method, no terminology, no system-based exclusions, barely enough description for a paragraph, and a striking similarity to the "theory" that all thoughtful persons live by when their common sense has developed into high awareness of their surroundings. True theory on the pattern of science is paradigmatic—it sets up models; history and criticism are empirical, *philophenomenal* (what pedantry does theory call forth!); that is, criticism and history continually invoke, instead of abstractions, experience.

Between the cultural critic and the cultural historian there is only the difference of the subject matter and its size. But just as the critic who deals with contemporary works adopts (or ought to adopt) a less decided tone, lacking as he does much of the knowledge that he normally relies on for interpretative assurance, so the cultural historian who assesses the state of civilization around him does so with the understood reservation that he sees no more than his incomplete sources disclose.

But, it may be asked, why should the historian venture to perform a task bound to be partial in both senses? The critic is needed in order to sort out current production, but the historian can wait until we are all dead and our full selves appear. This objection ignores the duty that goes with knowing something of the past. The cultural historian's motive is not the dubious pleasure of fault-finding. Rather, it is to reaffirm and perhaps strengthen what he thinks valuable in the activities of the culture makers, who are always subject to the distracting forces of fashion and competition.

The situation today—that is, the state of culture during the past half-century—holds for the conscientious critic-historian both temptations and responsibilities. He cannot help seeing signs that he takes to mean the end of the high creative energies at work since the Renaissance. Corresponding efforts today seem violent rather than energetic and their goal appears to be no longer the making of things but their unmaking—by travesty, pastiche and parody, and the allusive kind of art that relies solely on design, sense-appeal, and shock.

Faced with these offerings (and knowing or guessing their motive) the historian asks himself whether to encourage this wholesale destruction of meanings and emotions and thus help clear the ground for the new, or whether to lead a rear-guard action against the vandals, pointing out that the name of art is being promiscuously applied to mere facsimiles and parodies.

On reflection it is evident that the destroyers need no encouragement; theirs is the accepted style and tone; it prevails not in coteries but in the market. So the second role may prove more useful in the long run, provided it is strictly played: "guardian" must not mean bewailer, still less advocate of a return to anything whatever. The critical office is simply to compare pretension with performance so as to preserve whole and clear certain words, meanings, and standards. Such an effort may reduce deception (and self-deception), abetted by theorists who waste their breath and bewilder the public in attacks on a past already vanquished and in predictions and requirements intelligible only to themselves.

It is useless to ask what the new art and culture will be like. The genuinely new comes only by concrete example. In any case, a critic deals only with the actual. On this principle, and in the present moment of dissolution, he can only say, like the Virgin in Chesterton's ballad:

> I tell you naught for your comfort,
> Nay, tell you naught for your desire,
> Save that the day grows darker yet.
> And the sea rises higher.

But again, this warning does not conceal a hope of reversing the tide. On the contrary, the cultural historian is a sympathetic witness, as eager as anybody to see the ground cleared and the new begin. It is for the sake of that departure that he continues to report events in the light of history, seeing to it as far as possible that they are called by their right names.

The
Bugbear
of Relativism

For several decades the word *Relativism* has served to explain whatever the user found morally reprehensible in the life around him. The term, both scapegoat and insult, has all the properties of a thought-cliché of the learned-sounding kind. It is in fact a gross perversion of a technical term, as well as irrelevant to the issues it professes to settle.

What are the occasions for its misuse? Innumerable: read the books by clergymen and lay promoters of religion, by publicists committed to a secular cause, by observers of the West's decline. Consult the daily news of multiform evil; browse among serious novels and draw conclusions from the actions portrayed and comments made. Discuss with school officials and social workers their besetting problems. Best of all, listen to the conversation of troubled spouses and parents: my friend steals my wife, and my cleaning woman my spoons; my children take drugs and tell lies; my garage mechanic cheats me on repairs, and my thoroughly bourgeois mother-in-law is a shoplifter and a malicious gossip. It is "all due to relativism."

On the wider scene, the professions have lost their ethics—doctors defraud Medicaid, lawyers abet illegal deals, while their trade associations draft code after code in vain. In big stores, where the employees steal by reflex action, the management accepts the loss as "shrinkage" and passes it on to the customers. Political candidates promise one policy and in office pursue the opposite—the one I voted for gave away my Panama Canal. Government inspectors don't inspect (for a bribe), so that on building sites the very concrete turns relativist: scorning rigidity, it stays soft and compassionate, causing the death of a dozen workers. Airline and other disasters regularly prove to have been caused by culpable indifference to rules, often compounded by alcoholism or drug addiction.

As for leaders of corporations and states, a fair sampling are in jail or on the way to it. The world spins on a crooked axis. Nations sign treaties and truces intending to violate them before the ink is dry, and they borrow money like needy students and brash consumers, with no thought of paying back. They know the bank, the lending nation "can well afford it." This, no doubt, is Poor Relative-ism. The banker, of course, lists the large default as continuing assets "so as to look good"—public relations, private relativism. In short, say the accusers, it is idle to talk of principles, values, standards. Since the decay of religion, the western world has adopted the motto "Anything goes." Relativism has conquered all.

This bugbear cannot be sheer illusion. When the word is not a mindless echo, what people feel and fear arises from a confused impression that anything which varies with time and place, instead of remaining the same through all circumstances, is a menace: it shifts; it is shifty. To hang anything of weight, you want a strong peg firmly held so that it may firmly hold. Thus Relativism is equated with general looseness, with unanchored judgment and unpredictable behavior. This is deemed bad, because, as Bacon said in his terse way about deceit, "It leaveth a Man without a Hold to take him, what he is." Society obviously needs such holds with which to challenge, reproach, condemn the transgressor.

Strictly read, the indictment is paradoxical, because Relativism properly means the practice of *relating*, of linking. The dictionary calls it "the close dependence of an occurrence, value, quality, etc. on another." What is relative is tied to something else: relative humidity is tied to pressure and temperature; one's relatives are inescapably linked to oneself and to one another, no matter how they may regard the bond. Relativism may pose difficulties, but looseness is not one of them.

Before going further, a deeper doubt than the verbal or logical forces itself upon us: Can an idea—a notion as abstract as Relativism—produce by itself the effects alleged? cause all the harm, destroy all the lives and reputations? I am as far as anyone can be from denying the power of ideas in history, but the suggestion that a philosophy (as Relativism is often called) has perverted millions and debased daily life is on the face of it absurd. No idea working alone has ever demoralized society, and there have been plenty of ideas simpler and more exciting than Relativism.

If we think of Nationalism, for instance, we find that cluster of ideas taking centuries to become a force and, where it triumphed, doing so only under favoring conditions. Surely the moralist should take in the historical situation entire. Critics of society, and the press that echoes them, have every right to denounce and demand, but their outcry would be more convincing if they spoke from a wider view of present-day culture. They could then bury the bugbear.

A culture may be conceived as a network of beliefs and purposes in which any string in the net pulls and is pulled by the others, thus perpetually changing the configuration of the whole. If the cultural element called morals takes on a new shape, we must ask what other strings have pulled it out of line. It cannot be one solitary string, nor even the strings nearby, for the network is three-dimensional at least. To find not a single cause but these converging conditions, we must therefore look first at the persistent desires of western civilization for the past seven decades. We then see the worthiest endeavors—art, science, social science, education, human rights, criminal justice—like the least deliberate attitudes expressed in speech, manners, and dress, helping to do the work of looseness attributed to the quite innocent Relativism.

But the true role of relativism (and of religion, its supposed cure) must also be examined. Consider, to begin with, how inescapable the relative is. Through the senses, it is embedded in all our words and modes of thought. What is "hot"? The liquid that is too hot for our hands feels grateful to our face (as every barber knows), and we want it still hotter for a good cup of tea or coffee. All our ideas of size are relative. The bluebottle fly is a big fly and a wren is a small bird, though the wren is very much bigger than the fly.

Swift based Gulliver's successive voyages on this relativism of size, Newton his celestial mechanics on the relativism of motion. It is the imperishable glory of science that it discovers the ways of the universe by relating things in pairs, measuring the ratio, and then relating the relations in an ever-enlarging unity. Anyone who makes for himself a scheme of life does the same about things not physical—elaborately if he is a philosopher, and the rest of us haphazardly. For as Cardinal Newman said in defining education, "Not to know the relative disposition of things is the state of slaves or children."

Accordingly, ever since the great surge of exact science in the seventeenth century, the workaday world has subjected its doings to ratios expressed in percentages; it has "indexed" everything from taxes to summertime discomfort—all measures of something relative to something else. Unfortunately, in human affairs such as faith and morality, the facts are not amenable to numbering. It is impossible to isolate the elements; they are separable only in thought, and even there they slip out from under definitions and defy measurement. Misrelating is thus an ever-present danger.

At this point we touch the crux of the issue labeled relativism. The party of religion and the absolutist thinker posit the existence of "those great unchanging rules of life and conduct, eternally fixed and as old as the world itself." This code has one commandment for each offense, and the charge against relativists is that they vary the rule, depending on circumstances—"situational ethics." The charge rests on a distinction without a difference. For the absolutist ignores his perpetual predicament: his single rule will not cover all the actions it is supposed to govern. Make "Thou shalt not kill" an absolute, and at once conscience asks: What of self-defense? the death penalty? war to recover the Holy Land?

This last query brings us to the historical record of morals in the periods called religious. Standards in those ages, it is assumed, were both fixed and clear, a universally recognized system enforced by church and state. Unity and harmony of precepts strengthened individual and collective morality. Henry Adams found this view of the Middle Ages alluring by contrast with "20th-century multiplicity."

But actual life was far from answering to the summary description. Clergy and laity recited the commandments more often than we do perhaps, but popes urged crusades; bishops in armor fought and blessed massacres in local wars; priests and friars broke their vow of chastity and poverty; and abbots and towns struggled for gain in lands and power as steadily and ruthlessly as competing nations, corporations, and individuals do today. The repeated cry of the medieval moralist was "corruption" and "reform," familiar words that need no interpreting for us. The scarcity of saints is of all times.

Indeed, on reflection we may well think that the moral climate prevailing now in the West is in many respects superior. Politicians and churchmen do not seize neighboring counties by fraud or eliminate their rivals by poison. At worst, they earn illegal fees for using their influence in business deals—and for this we can blame the telephone. Besides, if fairness and kindliness to fellow human beings are signs of moral feeling, the laws and habits of the West in the twentieth century are infinitely superior ethically to the practice of the great ages of religion.

Take as a fair sample an era of reform, the Reformation itself. What does it show? The Christian faith revived, genuine religious fervor sweeping the masses of Europe, on all sides of the many schisms that the faith itself provoked. That same passion, coupled with intellectual and material aims, unleashed energies in leaders and followers that produced appalling results for 150 years: deceit, treachery, pillage, rape, and sudden death became the daily fare of the peoples, interrupted by brief local truces.

Much is made these days of the decay of private morals, meaning by this sexual behavior. And it is widely believed that before religion lost its hold on the minds of vast numbers of men and women, piety controlled the fleshly appetites. But medieval literature does not bear out that view. The sins of the body were not treated harshly by a church that had organized the system of confession and penance, dispensations and indulgences. Dante in his Christian epic is anything but harsh about Paolo and Francesca's adultery. It was not until Calvinism gained control of the state that the contrary attitudes called Puritan came into being. Luther himself was broad-minded about desire for "young girls with white legs." He restored the right of priests to marry so as to reduce the virtually conventional concubinage, and when the Landgraf of Hesse, feeling scruples against taking a mistress, appealed to him for permission to marry a second wife, Luther found that polygamy was authorized by scripture and gave his consent—though recommending secrecy. When rumor spread the truth, Luther advised "a big bold lie."

Examples without end could be cited to show such variations in the "eternal laws." They would also show that the changes were relative to conditions. It was the devout Pascal who pointed out that truth on one side of the Pyrenees is error on the other. And the truth on either side will shift. No clearer instance is needed than that of usury, by which the Middle Ages meant taking or paying any interest whatever for a loan. It was deemed a heinous crime and in various periods and places was punishable by death. The reasoning was biblical and clear. In a purely agricultural society, money does not beget money as seed and animals beget their kind. To exact interest was therefore to take cruel advantage of another's want, particularly in times of famine, which were frequent.

But as trade revived and joint-stock expeditions to the East prospered (see *The Merchant of Venice*), it became clear that money *could* beget money, and the church began to find uses and excuses for usury. It was said to compensate for risk, or for temporary deprivation of use. Wealthy churchmen were soon borrowing money at interest to enlarge their lands, or lent it to dispose of surpluses when feudal dues came to be converted to cash. Finally, the sin of usury disappeared, up to an agreed five or six percent.

When civilization becomes more complex socially and economically, it also becomes more self-conscious and more imaginative, and it perceives the need of making its dictates less rigid and uniform. Ethical norms can no longer be couched in declarative sentences; they adopt the form "If . . . then." Thus the early modern period saw the rise of casuistry. Acute and worldly minds among churchmen wrote treatises to guide the laity in difficult cases, whence the name. It was situational ethics replacing rigidity. Casuistry only acquired a bad name when it grew so subtle as to appear quibbling or equivocal, which is where absolute commandments lead. The person who is resolved never to tell a lie ends up searching for words that do not misstate the truth yet conceal it and mislead, as in the famous recommendation by the kindly priest regarding the lazy youth seeking employment: "You will be fortunate if you can get him to work for your firm."

One great sustainer of moral action is the law, and the law, working case by case, is an elaborately casuistical system. Theft is not theft, or homicide homicide, in absolute terms: in the one, mode of entry, use of violence, and temptation modify the crime, and with it the punishment. In the other, provocation, intention, accident, and self-defense abate the evil of identical acts. It is a riot of relativism. The law has also institutionalized another anti-absolutist notion in its view of the "first offender," not, presumably, to encourage beginners. Likewise, the parole for model prisoners does not imply a loose interpretation of the original sentence. Both are applications of the Christian principle of repentance, which is itself a piece of relativist judgment in the teeth of an absolute fact.

Generally speaking, the view of human life that a religion holds, coupled with the people's view of human weaknesses and strength, governs the amount of emotion attached to moral rules. Hence the disparity in codes, which does not mean that tribes and nations can exist without them, but that the danger and the horror felt about the items on the list are not immutable. In its Old English meaning, *murther* is a fine levied on the community after one of its members has killed a man. And in the early custom of the Eskimos, the (rare) murderer was only expected to move away and join another tribe.

At the other extreme, Puritan feeling did not merely decree total orthodoxy and absolute marital fidelity; it also charged with moral revulsion a long schedule of activities, to this day not everywhere repealed: dancing, the theatre, playing cards, working on one or another day of the week, swearing (even taking an oath), sporting bright clothes, using buttons—or the pronoun *you.* No Protestant sect adopted *all* these prohibitions—variation again—but one could paraphrase Pascal's saying: No card playing on one side of the avenue, bingo on the other.

Nor should the spectacle be dismissed with the word *Fundamentalist.* Till quite recently, enlightened England was certain that marriage to a deceased wife's sister was a sin—a species of incest. Within living memory divorce could wreck reputation, and remarriage afterward amounted to bigamy. Only a few years ago at a western university, a respected scholar was declared unfit to teach, because he had fallen into the habit of taking coffee at breakfast and had permitted himself the luxury of a vasectomy. Conscience is ruthless in its poetic power to make anything a symbol of righteousness.

This overvaluation of deeds and abstentions has repeatedly made the great religious leaders impatient. "We magnify the problem of evil," said Ralph Inge, dean of St. Paul's, "by our narrow and exclusive moralism. There is no evidence that God is a merely moral

Being." Again and again in Christendom, the purest religious thought has always proclaimed the opposition of religion and morality. Luther thundered against the idea that a perfectly moral man had earned salvation. And others down to Henry James, Sr., have pointed out that morality is divisive—it judges and condemns; religion forgives and reunites the sinful race. Morality strives for justice; religion for mercy. We are told that there is more rejoicing in heaven over a repentant sinner than over a steadily good man. This is reassuring to the former but hardly "supportive" of the latter; we have no record of what the brother of the prodigal son thought of the fatted-calf celebration.

Present-day moralists, who justly deplore contemporary vice and crime, should therefore revise their diagnosis. The alliance they regret having lost is not between morals and religion, but between church and state, which was at its closest in Calvin's Geneva. Elsewhere it was but fitfully effective in enforcing morality. And as these same critics very likely reject such a political tie, they must look farther for both an explanation of their dismay and the prospect of a change.

As to explanation, let me hazard a pair of hypotheses about the history of moral behavior; they may help to gain perspective on our own. It is a commonplace that periods of strictness are followed by periods of looseness. But what is it that tells us in retrospect which is strict and which loose? Surely the change observed is not in *morals*, that is, in deep feelings rooted in conscience, which are by definition hidden. The change is in *mores*—conventions, attitudes, manners, speech, and the arts: in a word, what the people are happy or willing to allow in public.

I suggest further that this change precedes the swing of the moral pendulum. This is not to say that the change is one of surface only, a shift of fashion among the visible upper classes. The public gradually accepts change under the pressure of social need or cultural aims, then comes the loosening or tightening of behavior in the lives of untold others beyond the fashion-makers. *Untold* is the word to bear in mind. For throughout every change the good habits of millions remain constant—or societies would fall apart; the bad habits likewise—or the police could be disbanded and the censors silenced.

The rise and fall of the narrow moralism that we call Victorian is a good example of the operation. It began well before Victoria's reign, causing such free spirits as Byron and Thomas Love Peacock to cry "Cant, cant, cant!" The new puritanism seemed—and was—a calculated hypocrisy; its aim, to control the impulses let loose by the French Revolution. (Revolutions may start puritanical themselves, but they undo and untie so much that they inspire the hope of limitless freedom, especially abroad.) To head off this menace, the English clamped down on self-expression, and perceiving that sexuality was the strongest drive to breaking loose, repressed and redirected its energy. "Respectability" effected the separation of love from sex, exiled the latter, and channeled human efforts into the approved modes of business, invention, church-going, and empire-building.

This remarkable feat is still vivid to us through literature and the fierce anti-moralism that followed, ushering in our century. But no period is homogeneous. Throughout the Victorian, the very high and the very low easily evaded the sexual and other imperatives. Artists and members of the professions periodically escaped to Paris or the suburbs. Dickens kept a mistress and joined Wilkie Collins on his trips to France, and Samuel Butler visited an accommodating seamstress. All the while, London was reputed the world center of prostitution, and in these equally moral United States the age of consent in more than one jurisdiction was nine years.

A century later, the anti-Victorian crusade of the 1890s has triumphed: we now have the New Man, the New Woman, and the New Morality that were propounded by Havelock Ellis, Olive Schreiner, the Legitimation League, and the Fellowship of the New Life. And these new ways conceal of course the "untold" sway of the old habitual morality.

This culmination of the new should cause no surprise. Ever since the end of the First World War, the slogan has been: emancipation. That war itself emancipated millions of men and women by throwing them into the trenches or the factories, dislocating lives and conventions together. Russian Communism then brought the utopian hope of an ultimate liberation. Freedom became an absolute good that must be extended to everybody about everything. Just as important, it must reign within the self. The word *inhibition* turned pejorative and accusatory.

In retracing the loosening effect of our century's generous intentions, it is hard to avoid giving the impression of disapproval. The implication is unwarranted. To describe is not to condemn, though it is understandable that to associate a proud achievement with a deplorable consequence will seem blasphemy to the passionate partisan. But in culture above all other domains, by-products, side effects are the price of performance. The history of modernism is rife with examples.

Deliberate emancipation began in matters of sex. Divorce was made easier and lost its stigma; "companionate marriage" (an American innovation) prepared the way for overt premarital sex; the teaching and technology of contraception gained momentum; and abortion was legalized. This so-called sexual revolution emancipated women even more fully than men, and a radical change in the idea and status of women, twice fought for in earlier times, now succeeded: they had the vote; they must also be free to lead the lives they wished. And logically and justly, all other downgraded, segregated, and neglected groups must be given the same access to a full life, a life full of rights.

The upshot has been to regard all barriers as outmoded and unjust. The ever-present impulse is to push against restriction and, in so doing, to feel intolerably hemmed in. Thus in practice, every liberation increases the sense of oppression. Nor is the paradox merely in the mind: the laws enacted to secure the rights of every person and group, by creating protective boundaries, create new barriers. The system as a whole grows intricate and uncertain: there is no telling what one may or may not do, for statutes take effect through bureaucrats who vary, since they usually follow not rules—God forbid!—but guidelines.

Besides, failing in one's duty is rarely charged with moral horror. Being law-abiding means filing a paper on time, not parking near a hydrant, and getting a zoning variance before moving a fence on one's own property. A world continually tighter in these ways intensifies the search for loopholes, tempts the unscrupulous to invent them, hardens the cynic, and keeps alive the urge to break loose. Such pulses of thought and feeling are bound to take away the ease and pleasure of ethical conduct. Habitual morality is baffled by the stop-and-go, and other people's disregard of injunctions causes no surprise; it seems rather to show firmness of mind.

This antinomian tendency began before the advent of the welfare state; for, as suggested, changes in mores precede the deeper transformation. The starkest contrast between modernism and the Victorian ethos is in the realm of manners, which have been well named "little morals." Respectability had relied on forms and on formality per se. So the informal, the casual broke out and began to rule. The stiff propriety of all ranks disappeared with the stiff collar and cuffs, the corset, and the tall hat. The new manners could be summed up in a material image: no starch.

But the soft collar and girdle and their even looser descendants liberate more than bodily tissues; they let loose emotions. By removing signs of class they also democratize; they offer open admission universally on the simplest terms, the culmination being the return to the medieval usage of first names at first meeting. The barrier of kinship, the privilege of intimacy come to seem "elitist."

The scope of the casual has indeed been remarkable. It has made room for the reduction of dress to a sort of primal dishabille on all occasions except burial. The barest, cheapest, and least assorted garments announce that the wearer makes no claim to special attention, that he or she is free of the conventional vanity that used dress to palliate humankind's physical defects. In its place sits the complacent belief that these never offend. Hair, finally, which has a long history of expressing the political temper, has been liberated from grooming and conforming to a common design; it is often left face-obscuring in the fashion of eleventh-century monks; though some use the freedom to express the ego through an elaborate hairdo. Noting all this, future historians will doubtless remark that just when the habit of coherent patterning called style was given up, the term *life style* was adopted to signify its opposite.

Stendhal liked to quote the maxim of his friend Mareste, *le mauvais goût mène au crime*, in which the "bad taste" that leads to crime refers to deportment, not to artistic preference. The connection is obvious, the link being self-discipline. One may know right from wrong, but acting on the knowledge is harder and presupposes a command of oneself that takes practice. Long before Mareste's epigram, Lord Halifax, the outstanding figure at the court of Charles II, observed: "Formality is sufficiently revenged upon the world for being so unreasonably laughed at. It is destroyed, it is true, but it has the spiteful satisfaction of seeing everything destroyed with it."

How much formality, what set of manners, promotes self-discipline without strain is a question for social philosophers and educators. The truth is that like any other art, self-discipline is rarely self-taught. Parents and teachers usually start the training, but an age of emancipation, rightly seeing discipline as a constraint, likens it to other oppressions and almost unconsciously loosens it.

Moreover, the scoffing at formality partakes of a broader, more intellectual attitude, which has come to be held in high honor: irreverence. Celebrities are praised in print for this talent, which functions like an absolute. The possessor ridicules all things on principle, showing thereby that he is not guilty of any unfair discrimination. True, there is another, perhaps compensating absolute, which is compassion. If irreverence betrays a strong mind, compassion shows a deep heart, and neither entails a moral judgment: Pope John Paul II is described as "very committed and very compassionate." The question "committed to what? compassionate toward whom?" does not arise. We are left to suppose that nowadays everybody is an underdog in need of automatic compassion from committed souls. For surely every social and political institution works against the individual. So let us steadily protest, enjoy the sweet taste of indignation, bask in compassion, and get revenge through universal irreverence.

It is more difficult to explain how in these times of image-breaking there should be so much talk of dignity—human dignity. The term denotes respect immediately granted, latitude within established limits for the person to act as he or she wishes, and an appreciation of worth, centered upon that person's best qualities. Therefore the modern zest for stripping and unmasking does not go well with dignity, which goes with decorum—with a façade that presents things at their best. Let suspicion or curiosity demand "the truth" or "reality" regardless of need or occasion, and dignity vanishes. Swift made the point when he declared impossible a parliament of naked men. On the day when a diagram of Dwight Eisenhower's intestines appeared on the front page of the paper, the presidency was something less than the day before. The press had discovered that a democracy has no need of dignitaries.

In keeping with this wish to be at ease, the press has been emancipated from the libel law; lies may be printed about public figures provided no malice inspires the deed; the "sensitivity" so loudly called for when groups are joked about is not required for individuals in the public eye. As for the great dead, biography takes care of them in the same manner, so eager are we for "all the facts" and so uninterested in their place or proportion.

Now, place and proportion make up the difficult relativism of fitness. It used to be called by its Latin name, decency, and was considered an ally of morality. When Henry James appealed to the "fundamental decencies," or W. H. Auden spoke of "a man of honor," they meant such things as the sense of obligation, loyalty, the security of the pledged word, the keeping of confidences and that form of self-respect which prompts the thought, This I do not do.

Such feelings have not died out, of course, but they have to struggle against casualness and the hatred of limits, even the self-imposed. It is now accepted that intelligence agents who voluntarily swear perpetual secrecy will break their oath after retirement and tell tales to enliven their memoirs. There's freedom of speech, after all. And what if this old notion of self-respect were a mask for self-importance? "This I do not do" surely puts a pompous emphasis on *I*, with overtones of superiority. The very notion of "it isn't done" smacks of outworn convention. *Anything* may be done. Irreverence is a broad mandate.

I said at the beginning that the dissolving forces at work were not of local or sectarian origin but have sprung from all parts of modern society. Like the casual reformers of manners, the deliberate makers of culture have powerfully aided the cause of liberation. If there is one domain in which "Anything goes" has been openly proclaimed, it is the fine arts. The absolute freedom of the creator, axiomatic for over a century, has produced masterpieces that demonstrate the value of the ever-new. But since original genius is not given to every artist, much spiritless contriving masquerades as innovation. There have been picture exhibitions "featuring" excrement, displays of "sculpture" including the nude body of the artist in a coffin, and the now familiar show of refuse found in city dumps or cast up on beaches. The counterparts in literature and music are also commonplace—scattered letters chosen by the throw of dice, incoherent dialogue, irregular tapping on wood, solemn silence measured in minutes.

Whether these "experiments" have point as reminders of raw sensation or prove that "all is absurd" is not the concern here. Nor does it matter whether manifestations of this kind are sincere. Provided they are visible and talked about, they set a new outward limit and confirm the lesson that pretty nearly anything can be offered as art and not be rejected or laughed out of court. The fashion may not last, but the stretch of acceptance does. Even pornography has come to flourish, because the wise refusal to ban it legally is seldom modified by the community's former reliance on decency: there is a fear of showing stuffiness.

From another quarter, the academic disciplines have with the best intentions thrown doubt on discipline itself. "Don't repress!": to crush impulse and desire breeds formidable retribution. This sound doctrine dates back to Blake, Rousseau, and Rabelais, but it is difficult to apply, and the injunction to relax usually takes effect as neglect—scamp the work, forget civility and common duty.

In this particular loosening, psychology (especially the kind claiming "depth") is seconded by anthropology through its reports of Samoan or other primitive peoples leading a life free of compulsions and therefore peaceful and happy. How unfortunate that its conditions cannot be reproduced in the West! With us, the worst oppression is that exerted by a mass-directed society. Social compulsion has never, perhaps, been so insistent and irresistible. All the means of communication convey it, as news and as advertising, and sociology gives it added power: "Sixty-two percent of those studied and followed up were found to . . ." do this or that. Who can withstand the lesson of the graph? The figures in the sample really mean the whole nation pitted against one person. Who are you to resist the majority? As Lady Bracknell said in Wilde's play: "Statistics are laid down for our guidance." A joke then, it is a rule of life now. And indeed it turns out that schoolchild sex and pregnancy do not really betoken a joyful, reckless moral holiday; they result mainly from "peer pressure."

From the early days of the century, "educational research" began its work of liberating that same schoolchild. True in far too many institutions, young bodies and minds had been virtual prisoners under torture. Children, as reformers have said for centuries, should learn out of native curiosity sustained by sympathetic teachers. In progressive schools, this self-governing idea was extended to allow the class itself to design its daily program, to learn only in answer to needs, and to evaluate its achievement without competitiveness. Grades were invidious; each pupil's performance must be psychologized in terms referring to him or her only. The corresponding scheme in college was the free elective system based on each person's tastes. Soon, a required curriculum came to look like oppression and obscurantism, another barrier to free development, not to say a violation of civil rights.

Home training followed suit. The theory of parenthood became simply: "Hands off." The child's psyche must not be bruised; no parental views must be imposed; wishes must be gratified to the fullest extent possible. One happy consequence has been that a child no longer walks in fear of his parents. But often it is they who tremble before the progeny's displeasure. With fewer and fewer demands at home and at school, self-discipline develops by chance, and born bullies in the classroom turn it into a kind of frontier society.

In keeping with this headlong march to freedom, linguistics has proclaimed a new absolute: There is no right or wrong in language; blunders are a natural phenomenon to be respected like the tides. And literature has aided the good work by giving right of entry to words formerly excluded, by disregarding grammar and syntax in the name of creativity, and by exploiting the narrow idiom of those unfortunates who struggle and fail to express their thoughts. At the opposite extreme, James Joyce's portmanteaus show contempt for what Cyril Connolly termed mandarin speech and make the dictionary obsolete.

Nor is this the end of the high-minded influences tending to unshackle conduct. It might be thought that of all the forces in culture, physical science would be neutral in morals and mores. To be sure, the ologies just mentioned lay claim to being sciences, but this is not enough to implicate physics, chemistry, and biology in the great loosening process. It is from underneath both social and natural science that this loosening comes, through the teaching of universal determinism. For although determinism may not always destroy the belief in responsibility, it muffles it. By whispering "How could I help it?" conscience is assuaged: the real agent is the unconscious, a dominant mother, a bad environment. Something beyond control does all the mischief.

This view has largely altered criminology. The boldest practitioners have said that crime could not be studied and treated unless the idea of responsibility was entirely abandoned. The true causes would then appear: poverty, broken homes, fixations, and other predestinating facts. In the courtroom, too, the expert has introduced similar opinions, so that in the end nobody seems able or willing to say at which point deliberate, responsible action occurs.

Lastly, for those who are skeptical about social and psychological causation, substitute forces may be found in the ideas of biologists and physiologists—"man a chemical machine," the neurology of the brain and its two halves, and the endocrine system. Diet, hormone, or neuron—choose among them if you want to touch the real self, with its moods, memories, genius, failures, and "honest mistakes."

What then are we to say of our moral state and its future? In view of what has been sketched here, some might be tempted to turn upside down the original indictment and argue that so far from Relativism being the source of present-day turpitude, it is its absence that contributes to the moral disarray. In its place is found a series of clamoring absolutes. "Anything goes" is certainly an unlimited fiat, and the partisans of the various liberations seldom adjust their demands relatively to the other, conflicting social needs.

But reversing the charge would be to commit the twofold fallacy of the single cause and of the pure idea. It is unwarranted, as we saw, to blame the decline of religion for misbehavior, and equally unjust to blame the faith in social betterment, which has in fact created a world that is in endless ways morally superior to that of one hundred years ago. The things that Western civilization has striven for and achieved had their origin in conditions rightly felt as intolerable. Greater choice in politics, economic life, in social and sexual intercourse were rational goals urged by some of the best men and women of their time. They foresaw and conquered difficulties, but not the consequences.

Of these, the most disconcerting is that the desire for a better society has generated a neutralizing power in the form of high individual selfishness. Throughout our culture, the most visible trait is concentration on what is owed to the self. This characteristic appears in the proliferation of "rights" and the freedom of the artist to please only himself; in the demand for faultless performance by physicians and manufacturers; in the principle of consumerism promoted by the advertiser: since everybody deserves to have all the new enjoyable, life-enhancing articles, one owes it to oneself to get this one at once. And with the usual paradox of freedom proffered, the gift coerces: "Don't be left out of the parade of pleasure."

Are we therefore peculiarly vicious and, as the cliché goes, materialistic? Certainly not. Greed is of all times and places. But today, two conditions make for a permanent state of self-seeking. One is the sheer number of other people. They not only obtrude, challenging or elbowing past, they also clog the channels and frustrate the arrangements that exist to ensure fair play and common rights.

The second condition is the burdensome legacy of the last century. We have inherited its methods of governing and of making goods and we have spread wide their results for our comfort. But the very thought of this double duty weighs us down with a great fatigue. Our forebears gave up everything to produce; we are determined to enjoy, and to see everybody sharing the bounty. Our weariness takes us even beyond the discarding of decorous habits and formal ways. We chant the maxim "A rule is only made to be broken." We want to deregulate work—no longer nine to five but at one's convenience. We have deregulated meals—no set times but eat-as-you-go, snack as you please. And for release we have augmented the dull solace of nineteenth-century alcoholism by the ecstasies of drug addiction.

Besides, the daily arrival of novelty tends to disturb moral habits and beget moral questions, usually dilemmas that oppose self and society. During the last World War, when men of science for the first time risked spying for conscience' sake, E. M. Forster wondered whether, if asked to choose between betraying his country and his friend, he would have the courage to choose betraying his country. A generation earlier or later, he would have felt no hesitation. Earlier, allegiance to country—other people—was sacrosanct. Today this patriotism seems ridiculous; let the country take care of itself. Accordingly, individuals exercise the "right" to visit the enemy in wartime; others are exempt from saluting the flag; and government recruiting for the secret service is regarded as besmirching the academy. The individual and his conscience have taken precedence over the claims of the community.

At the same time, self-regarding decisions can hardly be allowed in the new situations created by advanced technology. Artificial insemination, surrogate parenthood, prolonging life by a scaffolding of facsimile organs and fluids, altering genetic structures, interfering with the nicotine habit, compulsory testing to limit sexually contagious diseases—all these acts impinge on the community as well as on each person separately. Like abortion, these new practices threaten rights by pitting them against each other—the unborn child's versus the unwilling mother's. What is the consensus on the moral quality of those acts? There is none and perhaps none will ever be reached. But expressions of majority feeling through legislation will come, and it is safe to say the statute will not utter an absolute Yes or No. Conditions will be set relatively to which one or another procedure will be legal or illegal. We shall be indebted once again to a more or less intelligent and wise relativism: removing a life-support system may be made legal after brain death. When does brain death occur? How is it known? Who initiates the test?— three contingent decisions.

In these awesome moral ambiguities, scruples will remain to haunt the person making a choice. And it would be a mistake to think that when morals are flouted right and left today, transgressors are not beset by scruples; they agonize in the face of alternatives, of which one is ethical and the other excessively harsh. A revealing remark was made in a recent discussion of cheating on examinations. One student earnestly argued that not cheating showed "immaturity." The word was a glancing blow at the credentials system that rules professional careers. Failure to get good grades means a poor start, which may doom one to middling success through life. Since examinations are at best chancy things, one owes it to oneself to improve the chances. Not to do so is unsophisticated, immature.

This kind of judgment no doubt resolves a host of varied self-searchings. The reasoning in no way justifies the offense, but it condemns the arrangements that lead to it. In a society tolerant of attacks against "meritocracy" and always ready to lower standards in favor of equal treatment, the ambitious and able come to practice ruthlessness. White collar crime is the parallel to street violence, both encouraged by impunity, while the glaring injustices ground out by a paralyzed criminal court system serve as a perpeutual enticement. Plastic, the ubiquitous material, seems the perfect symbol of our state; it is at once stiff and pliable; it does not fit smoothly, but force it and it will stretch and hold—until it breaks.

How this sort of society arose out of the highest humanitarian intentions seems fairly clear. All social actions fall within one of three domains—in one, they are wholly free, because they are harmless; in the next, they are forbidden by law because they are harmful; in the third, they are free or not free according to custom and circumstance. In modern times, by deliberate thought, this third realm has been invaded and narrowed on the ground that the former customs were arbitrary or unjust. Liberation from them enlarged the first domain, that of wholly free behavior. But to guarantee this new freedom it was found necessary to move back more and more actions into the middle territory of the prohibited.

The modern citizen has thus lost two kinds of freedom, as well as the guideposts marking their boundaries, and he is perpetually tempted to recover what he can, a wanderer in no man's land. If he is ethical by instinct and training, he finds little scope for intelligent moral choices, let alone habitual ones. Right and wrong often appear on the same side of a recurring dilemma, while the worth of the things to be compared baffles judgment and defeats conscientious relativism. The moral person can only await the swing of the pendulum.

Exeunt the Humanities

Ah, the humanities! Everybody pays lip service to their worth; everybody agrees there is no finer sight than a full-blooded humanist; but the students don't seem to get humanized by contact with humanistic subjects, don't elect them en masse, and the prevailing but covert opinion is that the humanities are only for those who mean to make a career in one or another of them.

If that is true—and I have good reasons to think it is—then it must be that the caring for the humanities during the long stretch of their public agony has been wrong. But whence this wrongness? To begin with, are we sure we know which *are* the humanities? Usually, the study of language and literature; the history of the arts; philosophy; and sometimes history, sometimes not, depending on the whim of social scientists—it really doesn't matter. This threefold division—science, social science, humanities—which is convenient for academic organization, contains the germ of the evil that has infected nearly every attempt to revigorate and derive benefit from the humanities. By becoming "subjects" grouped over against other subjects termed nonhumanistic, the humanities inevitably become specialties like those other subjects. And thus their original purpose has been perverted or lost.

So true is this that the latest type of study in literature and the arts is purely technical. One studies poetry and fiction or art and music not to receive and enjoy a message, but to apply one or another complicated method, a method through which feeling and pleasure and meditation are pretty well excluded. As specialist practices these "approaches" as they are rightly called (for they do not reach the heart of the matter) may or may not be suitable for students who mean to specialize in this or that once-upon-a-time humanistic subject. Their value is not the point. The point is that if the humanities are made into so many social or other sciences, no humanizing effect can be expected from the transaction.

This assertion is really a concealed tautology, but it contains the principle that teaching the humanities to the nonspecialist requires the humanistic attitude. The teacher must extract from the humanities whatever they have to say about man, and the syllabus and department and dean and professional association must allow him to do so. This conclusion in turn brings unexpected discoveries. Listen to William James talking on this subject to a gathering of early American women graduates:

What is especially taught in the colleges has long been known by the name of the "humanities," and these are often identified with Greek and Latin. But it is only as literatures, not as languages, that Greek and Latin have any general humanity-value; so that in a broad sense the humanities mean literature primarily, and in a still broader sense the study of masterpieces in almost any field of human endeavor. Literature keeps the primacy; for it not only *consists* of masterpieces, but is largely *about* masterpieces, being little more than an appreciative chronicle of human masterstrokes, so far as it takes the form of criticism and history.

James's definition must be taken literally: "human masterstrokes" include the great performances of physical scientists:

You can give humanistic value to almost anything by teaching it historically. Geology, economics, mechanics, are humanities when taught with reference to the successive achievements of the geniuses to which these sciences owe their being. Not taught thus, literature remains grammar, art a catalogue, history a list of dates, and natural science a sheet of formulas and weights and measures.

The sifting of human creations!—nothing less than this is what we ought to mean by the humanities.

James's final exclamation does not entail our browbeating the science departments into turning humanistic, though some scientists already are, and more are willing to be. What James saw as a plain possibility has been partly fulfilled by courses in the history and the philosophy of science, where the creations of scientists are dealt with as parts of human biography and human cultural history.

But the lesson in James's words can be applied even more generally. It tells us that all knowledge may be put to two uses: it may serve an immediate and tangible purpose by guiding technical action; and it may serve more permanent, less visible ends by guiding thought and conduct at large. If we call the first the professional or vocational use, the second may be called the social or moral (or philosophical or civilizing)—the term does not matter. One is know-how, the other is cultivation.

Now for some hundred years American colleges and universities have innocently confounded the two, hoping to give their students the benefit of both. The double benefit is a proper aim. Both endeavors are worthy and both are valuable practically, but they require distinct uses of subject matter and of the mind, and they cannot be fused into one.

How did the mistake happen? At the turn of the nineteenth century the colleges were under great pressure—from the natural sciences, from organized business, from the growing technologies and the newly self-conscious professions. In addition, the new graduate schools were riding the wave of specialism. The undergraduate colleges somehow had to rejustify their existence. To play a distinctive role, they had only the liberal arts to cling to; so in order to placate both the social demand for professionals and the scholarly demand for specialists, the colleges broke up the old classical curriculum and invented the elective system. It was Dr. Eliot of Harvard who became its great exponent; he was a chemist.

As such, Dr. Eliot would naturally expect that a future chemist or geologist would take three, four, six, or more years of his chosen subject to become an accomplished scientist. But Eliot was quite content to see that same undergraduate take, outside his science, one semester of this and another of that for four years—perhaps four years of freshman work. The need to *build* a humanistic education in a controlled and rigorous way was forgotten, lost in the shuffle. The college curriculum broke into fragments and departments became small principalities competing for students and seeking prestige by specialism.

Not all thinkers about education made the same mistake. One of the perceptive was William James, another was John Jay Chapman, a third and the closest to the institutional trouble was the president of Princeton, Woodrow Wilson. In 1910 he spoke to the Association of American Universities in Madison, Wisconsin, on "The Importance of the Arts Course as Distinct from the Professional and Semi-professional Courses." He began by saying: "All specialism— and this includes professional training—is clearly individualistic in its object. . . . The object . . . is the private interest of the person who is seeking that training." This exclusivity he regarded as "the intellectual as well as the economic danger of our times"—an intellectual danger, because the merely trained individual is a tool and not a mind; an economic danger, because society needs minds and not merely tools. What Wilson feared was social and institutional ossification through set routines. He saw that "by the time a man was old enough to have a son at college, he had become so immersed in some one special interest that he no longer comprehended the country and age in which he was living." So it should be "the business of a college to re-generalize each generation as it came on. . . ."

That phrase of Wilson's is evocative and precise: to *re*-generalize, that is, to correct a recurrent fault. To that end he wanted "a discipline whose object is to make the man who received it a citizen of the modern intellectual and social world, as contrasted . . . with a discipline whose object is to make him the adept disciple of a special interest." He called for a body of studies whose goal is "a general orientation, the creation in the mind of a vision of the field of knowledge . . . the development of a power of comprehension."

With the aid of William James and Woodrow Wilson, it is easy to see that the humanities, the liberal arts, stand at the opposite extreme from the professional specialties, including the scholarship *about* the humanities—easy to see but evidently hard to remember. Why? Because the professional urge inspires the skeptical question, Of what use these liberal arts to the vocation-bent? Will they not resist the instruction or be spoiled by it? Neither James nor Wilson is the enemy of specializing or of vocational and professional training. The antagonism comes from the other side, the side of the trades and professions, and it has to be met head on. James did so in one sentence which has become famous, though it is not generally understood. He said: "A certain amount of meditation has brought me to this as the pithiest reply which I myself can give: The best claim that a college education can possibly make on your respect, the best thing it can aspire to accomplish for you is this: that it should *help you to know a good man when you see him.*" (By *man* he meant, of course, not male, but human being.) As he was addressing women, James added: "This is as true of women's as of men's colleges; but that it is neither a joke nor a one-sided abstraction I shall now endeavor to show." The development of his aphorism was this:

At the [vocational and professional] schools you get a relatively narrow practical skill, you are told, whereas the "colleges" give you the more liberal culture, the broader outlook, the historical perspective, the philosophic atmosphere, or something which phrases of that sort try to express. You are made into an efficient instrument for doing a definite thing, you hear, at the schools; but, apart from that, you may remain a crude and smoky kind of petroleum, incapable of spreading light. . . . Now, exactly how much does this signify?

It is certain, to begin with, that the narrowest trade or professional training does something more for a man than to make a skilful practical tool of him—it makes him also a judge of other men's skill. . . . Sound work, clean work, finished work: feeble work, slack work, sham work— these words express an identical contrast in many different departments of activity. . . .

Now, . . . since our education claims primarily not to be "narrow," [are] we also made good judges between what is first-rate and what is second-rate only?

The answer, of course, is Yes:

Studying in this way, we learn what types of activity have stood the test of time; we acquire standards of the excellent and durable. All our arts and sciences and institutions are but so many quests of perfection . . . and when we see how diverse the types of excellence may be, how various the tests, how flexible the adaptations, we gain a richer sense of what the terms "better" and "worse" may signify. . . . Our critical sensibilities grow both more acute and less fanatical. We sympathize with men's mistakes even in the act of penetrating them; we feel the pathos of lost causes and misguided epochs even while we applaud what overcame them. . . . The feeling for a good human job anywhere, the admiration of the really admirable, the disesteem of what is cheap and trashy and impermanent,—this is what we call the critical sense, the sense for ideal values. It is the better part of what men know as wisdom.

What this comes down to is the thing we today keep bleating about as "the search for excellence." If the motto is not hypocritical, it is certainly ineffectual. In higher education we give degrees that supposedly certify excellence and then require stacks of letters of recommendation in order to distinguish real merit from the rest. It has to be assumed, too, that among the letters there will be a truthful one to help us reach a sound judgment. And still not content, we also ask for figures based on so-called objective tests. In short we cannot tell a good man when we see him. Neither does the admissions officer, nor the personnel director, nor (all too often) the educated electorate. It may be said in rebuttal that judgment takes experience. True, and no less true is the fact that a humanistic education not only provides vicarious experience, but also prepares for the quick absorption of the experience that life delivers.

These several answers to the challenge, Of what use is the humanistic discipline? must be inculcated in the students from the outset. They must be made to see—or take on trust provisionally—that their studies are intensely practical. The humanities properly acquired will effect in them a transformation of mind and character which cannot be described, but which they will find useful all life long.

Just as important as making this prediction is to refrain from making false promises. Studying the humanities will not make one more ethical, more tolerant, more cheerful, more loyal, more warmhearted, more successful with the other sex or popular at large. It may well contribute to these happy results, but only indirectly, through a better-organized mind, capable of inquiring and distinguishing false from true and fact from opinion; a mind enhanced in its ability to write, read, and compute; a mind attentive to the world and open to good influences, if only because of a trained curiosity and quiet self-confidence.

All these things are likely results; they are not guaranteed. Life, like medicine, offers no certainties, but we go on living and going to the doctor's. So it must be said again: no exaggerated claims for the humanities, but a conviction in the teacher, in the department, in the faculty, in the administration, in the indispensable group of advisers, that this body of studies has a use—a practical use in daily life, even though no one can say, "I made a more effective presentation to the board because I've studied Aeschylus."

The next requirement is obvious but difficult: the course must be laid out and taught by humanists. They exist, but nobody can hire them wholesale. On the Jamesian principle of telling a good man when you see one, it takes a humanist to find another. This does not mean a search for geniuses. The need is not for transcendent talent but for an attitude and a pedagogical habit. Across the country at the present time, the departments of English and philosophy and history are full of very learned and very able people, of whom only a minority would be capable of teaching the humanities *as* humanities. The experience of half a century at Columbia has proved this empirical truth over and over again. In the courses in Contemporary Civilization and in the humanities, in the Colloquium on Great Books, some of those chosen to teach have failed, often from their own distaste for the enterprise, and just as often from the inhumanistic temperament.

Part of the reason for failure is that teaching the humanities cannot be done by lecturing or coaching or cramming. It must be done by the Socratic method. This is indeed the discussion method, but not as generally practiced. The true method is a directed and disciplined exchange characterized by order and consecutiveness. The instructor must not force the students' spoken contributions into a prepared channel, but he must, in Swift's phrase, "damp the pert and rouse the stupid," so as to cover the ground without letting interest flag.

The performance is conversation in the inclusive sense. It calls for knowledge, articulateness, sensitivity to words, courtesy, quick appreciation of the force of a remark, logic, and a steady awareness that the subject matter of the humanities is social in its genesis and its consequences. In the humanities, ideal Man is addressing other men *as* men and in endlessly different ways—through language in many idioms; through poetry, oral and written; prose discourse and the theater; music and the dance; political and forensic oratory; history spoken and written; myth, religion, and theology. All these activities, which we think were born inside college catalogues or faculty committees, are in actuality ancient social enterprises. Taken together, they offer to our gaze the total experience of humankind.

It is not possible through a college course or in a lifetime to absorb or even have a quick brush with this mass of crystallized thought and emotion. Hence the importance of making a wise selection from it when one wants to teach the young or the old what it has meant to be human. One has to sift human creations, as James said, and use the samples best suited to making a lasting impress on minds that are by age, training, or circumstance unaware of this treasure house.

The necessity of choosing is what led to the notion of the Great Books. It struck George Edward Woodberry at Columbia in the early years of this century; it was made into a course by John Erskine, then taken to Chicago and St. John's by Mortimer Adler and Robert Hutchins. The idea now flourishes with a life of its own, but it is by no means the only way to introduce the humanities. That *some* of the substance ought to consist of original works and not be descriptive or critical at second hand is obvious. It is better and more fun to read Shakespeare than a commentator and to listen to Beethoven rather than delve into the program notes. The determined, dyed-in-the-wool humanist can be trusted to fashion a humanities curriculum.

But it must be a curriculum, a sequence, not a batch of courses for picking over; and all parts of the sequence must be required, in the right order, over four years. Bits and pieces will lead nowhere—certainly not to a confident familiarity and a mode of thought. Nobody should expect a "humanized" graduate to come forth after a swallow of "world lit" here and a whiff of art history there. The very nature of the humanistic purpose excludes the elective system. The humanistically unprepared can only have hearsay opinions—or none at all—about what to elect and what to leave untouched. And again, the social nature of the humanities logically goes with sharing a common training and a common body of knowledge. Whether the curriculum is organized historically or topically, the training must be progressive and thus afford the pleasure of using increasing skill as each segment builds on the earlier ones. Of all conceivable subjects, the humanities are the least susceptible of being cut up and boxed off. Remember Wilson's desire to *re-generalize* the new generation.

When making his point about professional training as individualistic and the generalizing culture as social, Wilson unwittingly raised a political question that needs airing. All too often it is discussed in the vague terms of "democracy" and "elitism," the humanities supposedly favoring the latter and running counter to the former. Such arguments are foolishly inconsistent. A person is not a democrat thanks to his ignorance of literature and the arts, nor an elitist because he or she has cultivated them. The possession of knowledge makes for unjust power over others only if used for that very purpose: a physician or lawyer or clergyman can exploit or humiliate others, or he can be a humanitarian and a benefactor. In any case, it is absurd to conjure up behind anybody who exploits his educated status the existence of an "elite" scheming to oppress the rest of us. Humanists, as Wilson knew, are individualists too. As such, they are the last people to suspect of a conspiracy against the laity, which is all that is meant by the silly word *elitism*.

A more real danger than the imagined elite is our present combination of specialist and half-baked humanist education. The danger is that we shall become a nation of pedants. I use the word literally and democratically to refer to the millions of people who are moved by a certain kind of passion in their pastimes as well as in their vocations. In both parts of their lives this passion comes out in shoptalk. I have in mind the bird watchers and nature lovers; the young people who collect records and follow the lives of pop singers and movie stars; I mean the sort of knowledge possessed by "buffs" and "fans" of all species—the baseball addicts and opera goers, the devotees of railroad trains and the collectors of objects, from first editions to *netsuke*.

They are pedants not just because they know and recite an enormous quantity of facts—if a school required them to learn as much they would scream against the tyranny. It is not the extent of their information that appalls; it is the absence of any reflection upon it, any sense of relation between it and them and the world. Nothing is brought in from outside for contrast or comparison; no perspective is gained from the top of their monstrous factual pile; no generalities emerge to lighten the sameness of their endeavor. Their hoard of learning is barren money—it bears no *interest*, because in the strictest sense it is not put to use. One might argue that this knowledge of facts is put to use when the time comes to buy more rare books or silver plate or postage stamps. But that is not using knowledge to adorn life and distill wisdom, as all knowledge can be made to do when it is held and used humanistically.

I do not offer these remarks as an outsider who is scornful. I love baseball, opera, railroad trains, and crime stories, and I know something about them. But I am dismayed that others, who know much more, seem unable to do anything with it except foregather with their kind to match items of information.

All advocates of a humanistic education tend, as I have tended, to stress its all-importance as a discipline of the mind. It is formative, they say, rather than informative, and they urge teachers to remember that they should not be primarily concerned with expounding subject matter, but much rather with developing modes of thought and feeling. In some humanists it is even a kind of flourish, a gesture of pride, to add that they care not if ten years out of college a graduate has forgotten everything he learned there. To say this seems to mark off the high-plane humanities from the earthy grind of the vocations and professions. It is a ridiculous affectation. If a student really grasps what the humanities are and are for, he cannot help remembering in detail the successive elements that he built up into a cultivated mind.

The humanities, moreover, are a great vocabulary—terms, phrases, names, allusions, characters, events, maxims, repartees: thousands of embodied meanings with which it is possible to think and to judge the world. All these are facts, all this is knowledge to remember, accurately, intelligently. That being so, the humanities as a body of knowledge supply a common language. We cry aloud for "communication" and say we suffer from the lack of it. We ought instead to demand conversation, which pedants so seldom achieve. For conversation is the principle of the good society and the good life. It is the key out of the prison cells of our professions, our vocations, and our hobbies, and no less, of our fine arts and our scholarship.

A
Surfeit
of Fine Art

This year, in any year, the budgets of the federal and state agencies that support the arts are to be cut again. Meanwhile, costs in the arts are going up—rent, utilities, printing, and various incidental expenses. Yet one continues to read and hear of one more dance group being formed, yet another chamber orchestra making its debut, newborn theatre companies striving to lure audiences, festivals and exhibits being organized. Each new enterprise is self-assured of prestige, confident of deserving support, and hungry for subsidy from public and private funds.

This disparity between shrinking means and growing supply points to attitudes and assumptions about art that have not been examined for a long time. The most common assumption is that there cannot be too much art, and hence that the public has an obligation to support whatever qualifies under that name. If private funds fall short, let public money make up the difference. But since public money is not an elastic substance, some rethinking is in order, aimed at developing new standards of judgment and response.

The tendency to speak of Art with a capital A is the first cause of confusion. Art is not a homogeneous commodity, of which the need and use are self-evident. What the public is offered in the name of art is a multitude of objects and performances that differ in quality and in kind. There is popular art, supplied by entertainers who thrive without any subsidy. They are public heroes and heroines, well supported by worshipful followings. Michael Jackson has never applied for a federal grant, and Barbara Cartland does not need a Guggenheim in order to write her next book.

Another type of art—"high art"—is relatively *un*-popular, though it is very popular with its devotees. Auditoriums, museums, and theatres are usually jammed, and by paying customers, but not jammed enough to keep deficits at bay. This type of art, which has traditionally been a source of national pride, is also the cause of perpetual beggary. High art has *never* been profitable.

Today it depends on miscellaneous financing. Individuals and groups rely on the marketplace to provide at least part of their livelihood, but this must usually be supplemented by private patrons or public grants. Our large institutions use their endowments to pay part of their way, but they too require government aid. And then there is the art supported by colleges and universities. This last form of patronage is an innovation of our century and our country, a by-product of the artists' taking refuge in teaching when a widespread passion for culture took hold after the Great Depression. Campus art relies on both private funds (student fees) and public subsidy (state and local grants for higher education). In return, universities offer, free of charge, a wide repertory of plays, music, film, dance, and the visual arts that the market would never venture upon.

Off campus, the old, established institutions are in trouble, and show it: museums and libraries have entered the retail and mail-order business; they sell books, facsimiles of art objects, cuff links, ashtrays, calendars, postcards, and other reproductions of drawings and paintings. The New York Public Library rents out its lobby for dinners and cocktail parties; the Boston Athenaeum, besides running cruises to "art spots," let out its premises for the filming of *The Bostonians.* In Washington, the galleries of the Phillips Collection can be rented for the evening for $5,000.

As for the artists, most of them are periodically in dire straits. Seeing this spectacle, the art lovers are apt to lash out at what they call "our materialistic society"; it should pay for high art more lavishly. This double accusation is without merit. All known societies have been materialistic; human society exists solely for material purposes. Ours is unusual precisely in its generous expenditures for art, education, philanthropy, and other good works. Selfishness and philistinism are hardly our present trouble: some of the most fervent expressions of concern about the arts have come from businessmen and politicians. The former indifference or scorn has been replaced by concern and piety. When the budget cuts come, it is because of other pressing claims—the poor, the sick, the unemployed, the roads, the schools. In short, the trouble is not with the public opinion of art or the public outlay for it; it lies in the distribution of the funds, which has been guided—if the word is applicable—by totally unexamined ideas about "the arts."

Nobody who "cares about the arts" has dared to raise the question of oversupply. We are familiar with the dangers of too much farm produce, too rich a diet, too many births; we should also see too much art as a predicament.

An oversupply of art does not lower prices or cause the artist to go into "another business"; it only augments the need for subsidies. A museum or theatre rarely declares bankruptcy or moves to another town. It struggles on, in deficit and in tears, till rescued—for one short year—by a last-minute gift or a new commercial ploy.

Such is the fated result of an assumption deeply buried in our collective mind. It grew there early in the last century when the artist as a social type came to be glorified as a hero, a seer, a genius. Geniuses must be allowed to do as they please while the rest of mankind gratefully brings its offerings to the altar. We now feel the consequences of this potent myth. Because art generates excitement, because a great many people have some little artistic gift, and because the life of the artist looks wonderfully free, more and more people in each generation decide that they want to be artists. And throughout the land one or another agency is at work to multiply their kind.

Schools watch over every spark of talent and try to fan it into a raging ambition. The finger paintings of two-year-olds are put up on classroom walls and child poetry is publicly recited. This encouragement continues in colleges and in art and drama schools, where scholarships and prizes spur whole classes to proficiency. The résumé of any artist, or would-be artist, shows a string of awards, certificates, and commendations. Mastery of technique and native gift are no longer distinguishing features; they are the norm.

But the next phase is entirely unprovided for: where, how, can these talents find a social use corresponding to their preparation? The competition is intense. Young musicians, actors, and dancers form little groups, get a good notice, and immediately join the scrimmage for support. In painting and writing, the fight is to get into a gallery or a publishing house, only to be told that galleries are overcrowded and that poetry is not commercially publishable. In short, with the best of intentions, we have created a glut. Encouragement has bred expectation, and proliferating expectations have outrun resources.

Consider the glut in Greater New York. According to a report of the Port Authority, in 1985 there were some 117,000 jobs related to the arts in the New York metropolitan area, yielding a total income of $2 billion a year. What is the reality behind the figures? After you have counted the handful of well-known museums and theatres, the opera and ballet troupes performing outdoors and in concert halls, you must add the orchestras, native and visiting; the infestation of chamber music groups; the many libraries, public and semi-public; the almost round-the-clock lectures and poetry readings. In addition, uncounted other "distributors" offer their wares. The churches present plays and Sunday afternoon transcriptions on the organ of works written for orchestra. At the Cathedral of St. John the Divine, one can see a Miskito Indian fertility dance performed at the altar and roller skaters in the aisles enlivening the *Gloria* during the service. In the summer, there is free music in the sunken plaza of Rockefeller Center, Leonard Bernstein goes to Jones Beach to conduct yet another program, and Joseph Papp rewrites Shakespeare for sitters and strollers in the city parks.

One might argue that New York is a world capital, where a concentration of art is to be expected. True, but in many other cities and towns, as well as in "art parks" and converted barns in the open country, the high arts solicit public attention. Regional theatres are on the increase: festivals short and long resound everywhere— Texas alone advertises over two hundred. Art is ubiquitous in our lives: there is a piece of art in the anteroom of many business firms —an image to build up the image. There is art in good hotel and motel rooms, either original works or reproductions, such as the pair of Van Gogh sunflowers I once found, one on each side of a mirror. There is art at conferences and meetings: the sound of a string quartet graces a discussion of Niels Bohr at the American Academy of Arts and Sciences; and the annual report of a faculty club where the food is debatable boasts that in the last fiscal year the club sponsored two evenings of chamber music.

Already in 1840, Balzac noted with dismay that there were two thousand painters in Paris. Degas, fifty years later, said: "We must *dis*courage the arts." But the ever enlarging display of art cannot, of course, be cut or held back. We can pay farmers not to grow crops, but we cannot pay artists to stop making art. Yet something must be done. To lead people on when there is no chance they will ever fulfill their desire is immoral. And our training schools, art councils, endowments, and foundations are doing just that. They flatter the hope and belief that every good work and worker will be recognized and subsidized. When no such thing happens, anger and distress naturally follow.

Nor does the artist's anger refer solely to money. Government grants are awarded by persons (often themselves artists) who assume the role of bureaucrat. Their role cuts them off from the community of applicants. Subsidy, even by a private foundation, is an official act, and on this subject the French experience of three hundred years is conclusive. In France, the academic imitators got the commissions and subsidies; those who produced the works we admire today had to survive as best they could. The term *official art* means art that is competent and safe. As John Sloan said in urging government support: "Then we'll know who our enemy is."

Our current cultural attitudes leads to an oversupply of this competent, enjoyable art, satisfying but seldom great. At the same time, institutions of the highest caliber struggle to keep alive the masterpieces of the past and discover modern works of comparable worth. In the distribution of funds, both the producers and the caretakers are treated alike—and come out the same: disappointed and ill nourished. Only a change of policy, following a change of attitudes, can put an end to this demoralizing catch-as-catch-can. It would not solve an insoluble problem but might cut half of it away.

The first step would be to accept a distinction between "public art" and all the rest. Over the centuries public money has been provided mainly for public art and public institutions—museums, libraries, opera houses, orchestras, theatres, and dance troupes. All other artistic efforts have been supported by individual patrons and small groups of amateurs, or they have flourished quietly, locally, with no thought of wider recognition. Let us call this activity domestic art, because it corresponds to what people of an earlier age provided for themselves at home. Our mistake, our predicament, is that most of the art now produced is domestic art trying to become public art. There is no reason to neglect or look down on the domestic kind. But there is also no reason to support it with public monies. Its abundance is what creates the fierce competition, which in turn drives the truly public institutions increasingly to become gift shops, bazaars, mail order houses, and cocktail bars.

No doubt a certain number of those trained by our schools are great painters, composers, poets, playwrights, and performers. If they also have stamina, let them attempt a professional career. They will face a life of solitary toil and repeated disappointment, of problematic reward and fitful success. A few of them will eventually achieve affluence and world renown. In colleges and art schools the young should be taught what "the glorious life of art" is really like. It has not changed in five hundred years; it fills the biographies on our shelves; it is a test of endurance, willpower, and maniacal faith in oneself.

For the less determined, perhaps just as gifted, the practicable goal is to serve a local audience that is willing to provide a simple setting for the artistic activity, whatever it may be. This situation already exists here and there: small groups have been formed which enable composer, poet, singers, and players to come together and play old and new music for the enjoyment of the community, without fanfare, fund raising, or the compulsion to "go public." The baroque chamber music we play today with so much relish was once exactly this sort of activity, as unassuming as our chess or bridge, which no one proposes to support officially. True, these "private" artists would have to support themselves by means other than art and sacrifice any dreams of world applause. But as things stand, this ambition is sacrificed for them by oversupply. Many of them cannot even find work as teachers; the glut is there too.

With the activities of these artists redirected, regional culture would thrive, and its quality would be enhanced by the contributions of the more talented among them who now vainly try for the highest places. Nor would the denial of public money to such persons and groups be a stingy, meanspirited retrenchment. On the contrary, it would be a cure for the misery of many people, both artists and sponsors. By dropping the whole business of full-scale public exhibition and performance, private artists would no longer have to live the deficit and grant-matching life, struggling with costs of which the greater part goes in fact to stagehands, electricians, printers, landlords, and various profit-making suppliers.

The whole strength of public support—of taxpayers' dollars—would thus be freed to sustain public art, that is, the acknowledged public institutions. In each region these establishments are known to all, open to all, and subject to public criticism when their standards decline. If as a nation we hold the view that high art is a public need, these institutions deserve support on the same footing as police departments and weather bureaus. And I mean *support*, not meager help after periodic anguish and pleading. Public law has already recognized the social worth of these institutions by granting them tax exemption. The rest of their needs should be fully met, so as to free them for their work and take them out of petty commerce.

These suggestions and possibilities have nothing to do with trying to reduce the role of government in society. Nor do they relate to money alone, or artistic ambition alone. When I urge this new soberness, I am thinking of high culture as a whole and our relation to it. In the competition for cash, punctuated by elegant ballyhoo, in the overabundance of the offering and the fuss about it in print and on the airwaves, something has happened to the artistic experience itself. Its quality has been lowered by plethora. Great works too often seen or performed, too readily available in bits and pieces, become articles of consumption instead of objects of contemplation. They lose force and depth by being too familiar through too frequent or too hurried use. When I hear of someone's proudly "spending the day at the museum," I wonder at the effect: the intake is surely akin to that of an alcoholic. Music likewise is anesthetic when big doses—symphony after symphony, opera on top of opera —are administered without respite. We should remember the Greeks' practice of exposing themselves to one tragic trilogy and one comedy on but a single day each year. High art is meant for rare festivals, where anticipation is followed by exhilaration and the aftermath is meditation and recollection in tranquillity. The glut has made us into gluttons, who gorge and do not digest.

Such a condition disables one for judging new art. The eager or dutiful persons who subject themselves to these tidal waves of the classics and the moderns find everything wonderful in an absentminded way. The wonder washes over them rather than into them, and one of its effects is to make anything shocking or odd suddenly interesting enough to gain a month's celebrity. And so another by-product of our come-one, come-all policy is the tendency to reward cleverness, not art, and to put one more hurdle in the path of the truly original artist.

The Fallacy of the Single Cause

Among the American historians, Walter Prescott Webb holds a unique place as the man who saw in a vast tract of the western lands a culture distinct from that of the eastern regions, and who went on to explain its features by reference to the rancher's basic tools and their use.

That kind of intellectual performance is entrancing to witness. The magician's skill in pulling much out of little gives a soothing sense of logical unity, and that unity in turn sustains hope by suggesting that the chaos of the present is also order at bottom and will be so represented by some future student of our time. The demonstration offered in Webb's masterpiece, *The Great Plains*, seems to justify alike history and historiography.

The nature of these two related subjects preoccupied Webb as he worked—increasingly so toward the end of his life, when he wrote down some of his meditations. Their bearing is of course philosophical in the broadest sense. They touch on the character of human action and the lines of force within a culture. As such, these ideas concern not merely the professional historian; they are bound to cross the minds of the laity, even when not reading history. The ideas imply the question of cause—what makes things happen?—and its corollary: do ideas matter in the long run? In the short run they seem at once so dangerous (or they would not be attacked or suppressed) and so ineffectual (or nobody would dismiss them as "a mere idea").

129

Webb tells us that he had *his* great idea one night while he was still at work writing on traditional lines the history of the Texas Rangers. The great idea was this: two new things made possible the development of the semi-arid region he called the Great Plains. One was the Colt revolver; the other was barbed wire. The men who came out of the East passed from a forest region where the long gun, rail fences, and going about on foot sufficed to secure the means of livelihood. On the Great Plains, the size of the infertile territory required the horse, which in turn called for devices permitting self-defense and the handling of cattle without dismounting—the six-shooter, the lariat, and (for marking limits and raising pure-bred stock) barbed wire.

Armed with this idea, Webb spent a year in research, both to demonstrate that it fitted the facts and to discover what else had happened, what other changes in human life followed for Stephen Austin's colonists when, in Webb's words, they "crossed the environmental border" between the eastern terrain and the plains where there is no wood and never enough water.

Webb's first point about writing history is that it must proceed from just such an original idea. He congratulated himself on the fact that he had failed to get a Ph.D. at the University of Chicago and had never taken a course in the history of the West, so that he was saved from "parroting someone else's dogma" about the region he was studying. He was writing history, he said, "as I saw it from Texas," not from some center of learning.

In that regard, he was certainly in one of the great traditions. From Herodotus and Thucydides to Macaulay, Parkman, and Lawrence of Arabia, notable histories have come from those intimate with the ground itself and the life upon it. Webb was sure that his preparation had begun at the age of four, when he heard tales of Indian raids and massacres and observed, albeit unconsciously, the climate and ways of life.

For his method of conscious study, Webb credited a maverick Canadian professor at the University of Texas, Lindley Miller Keasbey—the only instructor for whom Webb had any regard, and one whose later dismissal by the university confirmed Webb's lifelong contempt for the ways and purposes of academic institutions. Keasbey's formula for understanding society was to start from the environment as a base and build upon it, layer by layer, the elements and activities of civilization, all the way up to literature, which is its fullest expression. When Webb was done, with help from seminar students gratefully acknowledged, he considered the work much too fine to be used as a ready-made dissertation for the Ph.D. that his colleagues wanted him to have.

From this first high achievement, Webb derived a theory of history as the product of climate and circumstance, a theory he extended later to account for the state of the nation in *Divided We Stand* and then to the world in *The Great Frontier*. Much to his credit, Webb explicitly rejected the claim of certain historians that their work can be "scientific." Rather, he said, it is tentative, incomplete, unscientific. True, the historian should be dispassionate, but he needs that "original idea" in order to relate the "forces, causes, and effects" that his research discloses. And to "give meaning to the past," he "seeks out the one pattern for special attention." These words are pivotal. He repeats elsewhere: "I worked hard in books to form a harmonious pattern which I knew beforehand was there."

I am not troubled by the apparent inconsistency of "seeking the pattern" and "knowing beforehand it was there." What is important is the combination of the environmental basis with the *one* pattern. He calls it elsewhere "the compelling unity of the American West." Compulsion means causation, and the search for the single cause of disparate phenomena is modeled on the aim of physical science. Webb acknowledged the fact when he called his great idea the "key" to understanding the American West and when he expected history to find in the past *an* explanation of *its* meaning.

It is also indicative that for Webb the root explanation was material—the soil and its climate. He attributed this postulate to Keasbey, as we saw, and later discovered that Keasbey had translated the work of the Italian academic economist Achille Loria, who in 1895 had written a quasi-Marxist analysis of Capitalism in which land and its relation to population play an explanatory role. Loria was cited by Frederick Jackson Turner in his famous essay on the influence of the frontier in American history, which Webb had not read when he wrote *The Great Plains*. What is surprising is that neither Turner nor Webb seems to have known of Montesquieu's elaborate theory of land and climate in Books 15–18 of *The Spirit of Laws*, a best seller of 1748.

But in Montesquieu geography is shown as one condition of historical developments, not a sole cause. The assumption of a sole cause, let me repeat, is a scientific idea—in particular, a principle of physics—which in the nineteenth century became an obsession in other fields than science. That is why Karl Marx, along with many other social theorists, looked for such a cause and all believed they had found it; that is why Darwin was celebrated as the discoverer of the single cause of evolution—and is still thought to have done so, although he himself acknowledged several causes. Darwin, it may be added, is one of the classic discoverers that Webb said he would wish to be ranked with.

The appeal of the single cause is linked with the conception of history as a vast process which overwhelms any individual will. The triumph of democracy in the last third of the nineteenth century certainly contributed to making that view prevail. It seemed self-evident when large anonymous masses migrated from Europe to America and within America to the West; it seemed confirmed when those same masses, by agitating and voting along geographical, regional, social, or economic lines, moved the nation in one direction or another. At such a spectacle historians gave up the earlier conception known as the Great Man theory of history, the idea which Emerson, for example, discussed in his essay on self-reliance and summed up in the dictum that "all history resolves itself very easily into the biography of a few stout and earnest persons."

These two preconceptions—of a single general cause and of resulting mass behavior—supported each other and led inevitably to the single cause being found in some material fact. The events of history could then be understood on a broad front, not as the conscious actions of individuals but as their reactions to a common condition. It followed that if the principle is sound, then by its extension to a wider territory, the development of a whole civilization could be explained. All its seemingly separate features would fall into place as outcomes of the underlying single cause. And since that cause continues to act, the future of the civilization may be predicted. This program of study and prediction is what Webb carried out in his second large work, *The Great Frontier*.

His mind may not have been influenced directly by the debate about history-writing that was going on during his formative years and preparatory work, but the ideas then discussed persisted "in the air." Dissatisfaction with earlier forms and methods was widespread and new goals were proposed. Lamprecht in Germany (and also in Saint Louis, where he came as delegate to the Centennial of the Louisiana Purchase) preached the fusion of history with psychology and social science. Others, such as Max Weber, wanted to find the historical constants of a period or movement, and Weber started on its long journey the notion that Capitalism comes out of Protestantism. In his careful work, the Calvinist ethic is only one of seven conditions, but later distortions left out the other six—the characteristic urge to find the single cause. In Werner Sombart, the genesis of capitalism becomes the identification of a single social type.

At the same time in France, a similar controversy raged for some twenty-five years, leading to the founding in 1929 of a journal called *Annales d'Histoire Economique et Sociale* and to the publishing of a series of books under the general title of *The Evolution of Humanity*. The issue in the controversy was whether history should deal at all with persons and events or solely with material conditions and widespread states of mind. In these last two the concern is clearly with physical causes and democratic feeling. This group of

French historians have been for half a century the models and the in-spiration for the majority of historians in every language. For the English, it was Lord Acton especially who gave the lead when in 1895 he said: "Study a problem, not a period." The only competi-tors have been the so-called psychohistorians, who have tried to be scientific in their own way, by digging below states of mind and ma-terial conditions to find in the unconscious the single cause.

In the work of the French historians and their followers, the in-dividual is banished from history. One scholar writes about "The Crowd from 1789 to 1848"; another gives "A History of Prices and Incomes." Lamprecht's wish has been fulfilled: the brand-new social sciences of the nineties have swallowed up history. But another element in the creation of the "new history" is generally over-looked. I mean boredom, fatigue. From the days of Scott and Ranke, the general public had been feeding on history insatiably, and by 1900 the young were tired of its contents—wars, politics, diplomacy, religious schisms, revolutions, and the great figures dominating the great events. Research brought out more and more details about those same old things; it was time to look at something else. The great historians had always paid attention to modes of life and states of mind, but the lesser ones gave the impression of being dry as dust.

The new-style history was not without drawbacks. It dealt with relatively narrow subjects, with extracts from the grand spectacle of history, and the evidence presented was trivial in character though massive in amount. The conclusions might be fresh and startling, but they could be put in a few sentences. The rest was material to consult rather than to read.

When Webb wrote a foreword to the *Texas County Histories*—a collection of 814 books and articles by different authors—he said: "The general historian who can synthesize them and tell the story of Texas with the same fidelity will have written the book that Texas is waiting for." The point of that remark is that he said the *story* of Texas. A story has a beginning, a middle, and an end. It has people with names, who act from recognizable motives toward an intelligible goal; and on the way to it, things happen: there are conflicts, disasters, triumphs, reverses, failures, creations, rejoicings, deaths, and rebirths. Browsing among the modern studies one wonders who or where Webb's "general historian" may be who will synthesize those fragments into the story of anything; and, supposing such a person, what chance there is that anybody will take him seriously when he disregards the prevailing conception of history and produces *a story*. In a current catalogue from a university press, under the heading History, there is only one work with a title suggesting a story. It is *A Political and Diplomatic History of the United States*; it is by a Japanese, published by the University of Tokyo Press, and merely distributed by the American publisher.

For the student of the past today, the task of composing a skilful narrative, alive with people and intelligible in form as well as defensible in detail, is daunting. To write a history seems more difficult than to write a great novel. And here comes the subtle temptation. The historian's research has accumulated many facts; his fellow workers have produced many monographs—"studies of conditions," social and psychological—which contain valuable analyses of slices of the past. These findings can certainly be incorporated into true history. But in the face of this vast heap, the writer may be appalled, indeed panicked by the need to devise memorable patterns. He is drawn, seduced by the idea of a unifying principle.

Webb was sure that after absorbing and reflecting on a mass of facts, the gifted historian would be inspired with an "original idea" capable of organizing all the evidence. The original idea has to be tested, but there is no need to turn encyclopedic and run after every fact. The great histories, he pointed out, continue to be read despite the steady piling up of new facts. What matters is the power of the idea to give shape, as a theme does in art.

Narrative history presupposes men and women whose motives lead to action and result in events. But we no longer believe in the importance, even in the reality, of active men and women; we think they are moved by other forces, of which they are not conscious— by economic, dialectic, material determinism; by a thing called "their society"; by the unconscious, individual or collective; or, as Webb decided, by the environment. These accounts put the motive power *behind* history and unmistakably point to the single cause. For no matter how much the narrator hedges by admitting lesser or secondary causes, the one he calls principal or fundamental is the one that drives the human crowd and commands the march of events.

The scheme looks so plausible: in an age of political democracy and mass culture, of world trade and interlocking industries, how *can* one believe in the Great Man and his directing will? The answer is, no need to believe in him, even though one has actually seen a few rather recently: Stalin, Mussolini, Hitler, Gandhi, Churchill, De Gaulle (great does not mean good). But leave them aside and forget the label "great." The question is not that of supreme power, and not even of power, but of action. When Webb attributed part of the explanation of the West to the Colt revolver, he was giving a role to an object that would not have existed without a man—Samuel Colt. There was nothing casual about the success of the invention. Sam Colt was keen about guns and explosives from his boyhood. His early design and business failed, and he very nearly gave up. But he persevered, helped by the onset of the Mexican War and, as a composite result of man and event, one of Webb's conditions was created. Nothing was inevitable, nothing fated in the sequence. It took numerous acts of intelligence and will and self-interest on the part of Colt and his backers before the weapon was produced, far from Texas; so that the object became, as it were artificially, part of the western environment. Revolvers do not grow in the desert like cactus, nor do barbed wire and windmills.

If it is argued that the environment produces the men who produce the devices, the generality is so indefinite that it explains nothing. To be sure, an environment and its culture, in the East, acted on Samuel Colt, but that setting had existed well before him and had not yielded a firearm usable in the West. Thirteen centuries earlier, another desert, in Arabia, "produced" Mohammed. But no visible necessity called for his appearance, the results of which down to our time have been incalculable. The presence or absence of certain human beings makes a difference—Joan of Arc by her actions crowned a king and helped unite a nation. Suppose William the Conqueror killed at Hastings instead of his horse; the Normans had no other leader of ability. Now leave out, if you like, all future English history, Parliament, the common law, and just think of the English language; it is inconceivable that without the Norman Conquest English would have been what it is today: Soil and climate did not concoct it. Individuals make a difference, though not wholly by themselves. Chance and others' wills set the boundaries of individual power, which is in turn modified by the particular scene. A true history is the tale of their continuous interaction.

To discern and make vivid this interaction is not simple; and when the effort succeeds, people want a bonus besides, an explanation. Webb's account of the Great Plains was the fulfillment of that desire. He went further and looked for the corresponding "key" to the entire course of Western civilization since 1500. He found it in what he called "The Great Frontier," by which he meant the Western Hemisphere and its vast material resources. As long as these were abundant, Western civilization here and in Europe thrived and was profuse in all kinds of creation, including the cultural. But by 1900 the frontier was beginning to close, and shortly the door would be permanently shut, with no other open frontier in view.

It would take too long to list the difficulties that stand in the way of accepting this hypothesis. The main trouble is that Webb's method of building the historical structure layer by layer, from the material base up to the fine arts, is not applied in his book with sufficient familiarity with the tone and character of Europe itself, the complexity of its history and of its leading figures. The treatment of economics at the base and of literature at the top are notably lacking in sureness of touch. Webb was out of his element, displaced from the post of vantage he so rightly valued. The American West, he said, he had seen from inside; it was for him an ideal region because it contained "no industry, no special institutions, no battlefields, no statesmen—only local politics, which are the least complex."

The Great Frontier nonetheless belongs in a discussion of history, being typical of the recurrent effort to frame a philosophy of history. An explanation of the past, said Webb, must supply its meaning. That conviction has produced famous works, from St. Augustine to Hegel and from Spengler to Toynbee, whose *Study of History*, by the way, Webb seems to have regarded with sympathy. But philosophies of history are not history, except here and there, when the author narrates events to prove his thesis. To put it differently, the search for the meaning of the past corresponds to the search for the single cause. They are the two facets of one idea which is inherently anti-historical.

For a philosophy, a meaning, is by definition a principle that does not accommodate exceptions. It is like a stencil laid over the map of events: only what shows through the holes can have significance, and unfortunately it is inevitable that what the stencil shuts out is often more important than what the philosopher needs in order to establish his principle or meaning. Does this imply that history is meaningless? If so, what about the "original idea" that helps to organize confusion? Well, *an* idea is not the same as *the* meaning. The organizing idea may serve well for a modest portion of the past, modest in geographical range or in timespan. There is then no need to suppress or belittle great chunks of reality. And the bearing of an idea need not be exclusive; it may be offered as highly suggestive, a pragmatic explanation in the technical sense of *pragmatic*. It is a view, a convenient pattern, a tenable interpretation, not a system or a stencil.

This difference enables the historian as well as the reader to feel free. The historian need not stuff ready-made cubbyholes, and the reader can enjoy what he reads without apprehension that the evidence has been scamped. Gibbon can affirm that the decline of the Roman Empire was due to Christianity, and Mommsen can show how disastrous for the Roman heritage Caesar's assassination was. Neither view coerces.

As for the "meaning" of the past, it is bound to be thin and abstract. Toynbee can be summed up as saying that there are twenty-one civilizations and that they were tested for survival by "challenge and response." Why read six volumes to find that out? The truth is that when the great Toynbee boom occurred, twenty-five years ago, more people bought the books than read them. Few who are not historians finished reading even the two volumes of the abridgement. Similarly, Spengler was understood from his title alone—*The Decline of the West*—plus, perhaps, his definition of Faustian Man, which anyone could learn from a good review of the work. The explanation in Webb's *Great Plains* is even easier to reduce to a formula, but fortunately his descriptive power and love of the region and its people make the work much more than the working out of a thesis.

Periodically, one of these abstract explanations gains wide publicity, either because it is startling or because the professionals praise and attack it. But what other, closer contact has the educated person of our century with history? At times, a subject, the massive research on which it rests, and some original feature in it draw attention to a work classed as history. As noted on an earlier page, Fernand Braudel's large study of the Mediterranean world has received wide acclaim. It fulfills the specifications of the *Annales* group by being quantitative about economic and social facts over a great stretch of time and territory and it presents patterns. But the figures impress us only by the rhetoric of numbers; traditional literary sources had told us as much—and more. For as a reviewer pointed out,

The mistakes and distortions which abound in Braudel's work are not so much incidental as inherent in his method, in his very approach to historical studies. For he will identify his long and medium-term patterns and cycles irrespective of events and policies, of political and military power. What confronts us in Braudel is a systematic disregard of the action of statesmen and the impact of alliances, treaties, and blockades. Occasionally, he stumbles awkwardly up against the fatal contradictions in his own method.

We catch a glimpse here of the inhumanity, indeed, of the anti-humanity of the method. It professes to deal with populations and states of mind, but by eliminating from the account the varying fortunes of individuals and businesses, of soldiers, statesmen, and diplomats, it presupposes under the surface of things the action of a great machine; it is the automation of history.

If I were asked where today the feel of genuine history can be had, I should say in the autobiographies of statesmen and military commanders. They cannot avoid being narratives, and they depict the confused interaction of many human beings, as well as the role of accident. Such a book as Dean Acheson's memoirs, *Present at the Creation* or Harold Macmillan's *War Diaries* are first-rate examples of what I mean.

To sum up, the value of history does not consist in explaining by formula, in "revealing" some potent principle that governs one or twenty-one civilizations. The value lies in the spectacle itself. The chain of events need not be long—Macaulay's *History of England* covers in detail only twelve years—but it must be thick with the deeds and aims of many individuals. These are always tangled and their meaning or "lesson" is simply that to other human beings the scrimmage is intelligible.

The sense of *how things go* will yield different ideas when the piece of history comes from ancient Rome, from nineteenth-century China, or from the United States in the 1920s. Therefore, these various settings, physical and other, must be coherently set forth. And equally important, the historian must choose a subject that is capable of treatment by pattern and chronology. That is why the political life of nations has been the prevailing subject of histories. The chain is unmistakably there. It is possible to deal with aspects—diplomatic or economic—or with single activities provided they are continuous: the history of baseball or of the fine arts. But topics that lack a spatial and chronological unity, such as "the history of the Irish in America" or "the history of Asia" do not yield books of history. The former subject has no continuity, the latter has no unity. On the same principle, there can be a history of feminism but not "a history of women." When the late Philippe Ariès wrote *Centuries of Childhood*, he supplied interesting vignettes of changing attitudes toward children, but he did not perform the impossible task of writing a "history of children," any more than he could have written a history of redheaded people. At the cost of repetition let this fundamental truth be clear: a history could be written of the weather in Marin County between any two dates, but not a history of the thunderstorms. A History of the Idea of Progress is possible and has in fact been written, whereas a History of Human Stupidity cannot be, plentiful as the source material obviously is.

All subjects suitable for history and treated *as* history are so many implicit denials of the single cause, as well as tonic doses injected into the body of a civilization. Beyond the pleasure of recognizing ourselves in the past or meeting remarkable strangers there, the reading of history, when widespread among a people, confers on them a power of which Webb was acutely aware and which he tried to describe for his students and readers. His words in that same preface to the *Texas County Histories* put it most movingly: "Books accumulate in the community, knowledge spreads about the community, and the people come to feel that they have a culture and a civilization of their own and not something borrowed or brought in for a summer trip. . . . We can never have real education, or a self-perpetuating culture, until we get beyond the description and the describer to the things described."

He meant that knowing history endows everything we see and touch with additional meanings—not a single overarching one, but a multitude of associations as real as the object or the scene itself. Life is made thicker, richer, of weightier import because other beings than ourselves—yet kindred—have passed where we walk.

License to Corrupt

The use of rhetoric in teaching composition and literature has had a long and, until our century, successful tradition. Criticism itself has often in the past come within the purview of rhetoric, making it altogether an influential branch of learning. Then the subject fell on evil days: rhetoric seemed to be no more than a bag of tricks taught and used mechanically. The dismissive phrase "mere rhetoric" meant words without substance. Applied to literature, it meant verbal effects without feeling behind them.

Today, rhetoric has made a comeback, but with a shift of object. Although the ancient word *rhetor* means "I speak," what interests the modern rhetorician is not the speaker, but the listener or the reader. Rhetoric now goes in for analysis and interpretation—and not just of texts; it seeks to probe into all our convictions. "The new rhetoric," says one devotee, "is not part of literature; it is concerned with the effective use of informal reasoning in all fields." Indeed, it claims a revolutionary influence on philosophy, psychology, and ethics. You do not have to look very far to find books and articles entitled the "Rhetoric of this" and the "Rhetoric of that," the *this* and the *that* being far removed from language. Since it is now the receiver that is being studied for shock and response, we may sooner expect a work on "The Rhetoric of Rheumatism" than any return to the kind of textbook formerly called *Grammar and Rhetoric*, which taught the principles of writing exposition, description, narrative, and argument.

In these conditions, it is likely that whatever benefits we are to gain from the new Rhetoric, it will not help us in the teaching of composition. The difficulties there are acute and they gravely affect business, government, publishing, and society at large. Everywhere, one hears dismay about the state of literacy—literacy in both senses: the bare ability to read and write and the developed ability to write well and understand texts. So far no theory, no analysis, no system has brought relief.

That discouraging fact has been observable for fifty years or more, and many contributory causes have been named. But I believe an important one has been overlooked. I have in mind the assumptions about language and rhetoric that have been accepted as valid and useful. The trouble lies in these ideas when translated into action.

The chief of these assumptions is that science is now in charge. In a widely used little book called *Rhetorical Criticism*, we are told at the outset: "All intellection aspires to the condition of physics." And the author goes on to blame older rhetoricians for being naïve and lacking the rigorous methods only now discovered. True, the author notes some differences between physical scientists and workers in literature, but these differences come after the scientific method has been established as the indispensable tool. The same assumption has prevailed in the study and teaching of language for nearly a century, so that by now the doctrines of theorists are taken not as tenable ideas but as matters of fact.

The steps by which these teachings gained power over the common mind forms an instructive episode in cultural history. Toward the end of the eighteenth century and the beginning of the nineteenth, the comparative study of European languages led to discovering family relationships, chains of etymology, and regularities in the change of sounds. Grimm's findings about the shifting of consonants was an achievement regarded as comparable to a discovery in physics, and it was called Grimm's law. In naming their work science, the linguists of that time or philologists, as they were called, meant that it was systematic and not fanciful. In every European tongue except English, the phrase "scientific work" still means just that. After all, the root meaning of science is simply knowledge. But by 1865, when Max Müller, the transplanted German lecturing at Oxford, offered a course on the "science of language," something had happened to the key word. Thanks to the agitation about Darwinism, science and scientist had become objects of worship; the older terms *naturalist, natural philosopher*, went out of use, and the conviction spread that nothing was true or sure except the findings of physical science. The adjective *scientific* became a judgment of value and a source of pride.

That was Act I of the cultural drama. Act II could be predicted. It was the scramble on the part of every scholarly discipline to earn or snatch the label *scientific*. Historians, sociologists, psychologists, anthropologists, educators, grammarians, even road builders and mechanics—all crowned themselves scientific in the new sense of purveying rigor and certainty.

In subjects related to language, this scientism was reinforced toward the end of the nineteenth century by an important social revolution: the new free public schools were turning out their products on a national scale. The resulting enlargement of the reading public led to the creation of the penny newspaper and other forms of popular literature, and this in turn drew attention to common speech, as against the rhetoric of high literature.

This shift, moreover, coincided with the replacement of the classics curriculum by the new sciences, which were touted as modern, concrete, lively, and practical. The traditional subjects and their literary sources were now called antiquarian and unpractical. The old grammar was denounced as not only schoolmarmish but unscientific, because it followed the outline and terminology of Latin grammar. The English scholar Henry Sweet, the model of Shaw's Professor Higgins in *Pygmalion*, published in 1891 a *New English Grammar* professing to be the first scientific one. The point was that the grammar would describe the workings of English, not prescribe any forms or usage. Henceforth there might be regularities in language, but there would be no rules. The efforts of the earlier philologists—Grimm's and Verner's law and similar findings—were replaced by direct, present-day observation of the spoken tongue. Accordingly, French, German, American, Scandinavian and other scholars began to go on their travels—at home—to observe and describe. This resolve and this endless field trip felt like an emancipation, as if these new scientists were at long last grappling with reality instead of convention.

True scientists—physical scientists—are not to blame. They gave up a good while ago the conceit and aggressiveness that marked their style while getting a place in the sun. Having won even more than that place, they now attend to their task with devotion and propriety. But what I have called the cultural pressure of science continues, energized by envy of their success.

Meanwhile, the public has learned the tenets of the new scientific grammar. Its first lesson about language is that it is a part of nature. A language is a living thing—except, of course, when it is dead. One sign of its life is that it is changing all the time, and it is an absolute commandment that no change must be interfered with; for, on the one hand, linguistic change cannot be resisted and, on the other, to repress change would thwart or stunt life. When the linguistic authorities write for the general public, they always speak with contempt and derision of efforts to guide or straighten out the language. They also tend to deny that during the life of a language it is at times better—more uniform, elegant, flexible—than at other times. For whatever happens to it is not disorder and decay but necessary evolution, as in the animal and vegetable worlds. Language twists and turns in perpetual adaptation, and at every stage is as it ought to be.

The linguist here is playing two roles. As would-be scientist he refuses to utter value judgments, and as a professional he is saying: "Hands off!" He thinks that if anybody meddles with his subject matter, by introducing the idea of right and wrong, the discovery of lovely new changes will be taken from him.

This twofold doctrine has captured the minds of those who struggle to impart the rudiments of good speech and good writing in the schools. It shapes the classroom behavior of teacher and taught, their common law being laissez faire: one word is as good as another and the child is entitled to use all the speechways of the home, for—who knows—an odd way of pronouncing or writing may in time become the usual way. Thus does language grow and thrive.

These precepts might be sound if linguistics were a natural science and if science were meant to control teaching. But the analogy with science is false. Language is not a living species that evolves by necessity. Only the speakers are alive. Without perishing themselves, they can kill a language, as history has repeatedly shown, by merely being conquered and taking up their alien masters' speech.

Besides, the would-be scientific description of a language is only an approximation. What the observer records is vocabulary, some grammatical forms, and some pronunciations. The actual speech of a whole people is beyond the reach of accurate description. It changes and breaks down every minute. Many of us some of the time and some of us all the time speak in incoherent fragments, with irrelevant words and noises thrown in, free from any recurring forms of grammar. Pronunciation too varies endlessly, not only from person to person but within each person's utterance at different times. And so far as I know, no one studying language has ever measured speed and spacing, which so strongly affect meaning and receptivity. It would be as easy to record the stream of thought of a multitude as to ascertain the actual, fluid reality of a nation's speech.

What is in fact done is to make up a schema from the partial data that can be caught on paper or on tape, and learn from it what we can. The results have been remarkable and of immense value. We know much more than was ever previously known about dialects, phonetics, slang, and the many other facets of that wonderful creation, language. But from the comparison of language to a living organism subject to necessity, a foolish faith has grown that a new word is created when it is needed, that an old one disappears when it is no longer useful, that the success—that is, the currency—of a new term corresponds to its merit and utility; in short, that everything works toward the best of all possible outcomes. If some convenient or subtle verbal distinction is blurred by ignorant mis-use, cheer up—there are as many good fish in the sea as ever came out of it.

That belief cannot help affecting the student and his teacher in their joint efforts to improve verbal expression. The one is com-placent about his careless error; the other is afraid to condemn it for fear of precipitating a cardiac arrest in the life of the mother tongue. No fault is serious because no fault is really a fault. This principle has been put by a leading authority in unforgettable words: "No native speaker can make a mistake." He is only remolding what belongs to him by birthright. The author of this view, Professor Allen Walker Read, is a colleague and esteemed friend of mine, but in the words I have quoted he speaks for the false religion of of the miscalled science of language.

Suppose we did have a natural science of language. What could we expect from it? First, it would cover with *increasing* precision all parts of the subject—grammar, syntax, vocabulary, pronuncia-tion and their various aspects. Then, the terminology would be clear, uniform, and universally accepted; there would be fixed units, known variables, and measurement of their functional relations. The upshot would be: prediction, that is, within well-defined limits, regular linguistic phenomena could be counted on to occur.

Language as observed gives no hope of any of these expectations. The terminology is individual and chaotic. The variety of languages does not favor universal systems, and its "life," which means change, defies exact mapping. Once upon a time, the phoneme was offered as proof that a social science could boast a true scientific unit, but it soon lost its claim. The phoneme is elusive, localized, impermanent, and defined in half a dozen different ways, one of them asserting that "it is not a sound but a bundle of relevant sound features."

The conclusion is inescapable: language, like history, like the human mind, belongs not to science but to the realm of finesse. New words do *not* appear when needed; centuries pass without their creation. Existing words do drop out when still needed and clearly used. The success of new coinages depends on vogue, which is largely accidental, like the success of a play or a book. As with books, a popular novelty suddenly dies, with or without competition, with or without replacement.

It is this strictly human waywardness, in speaking as in writing, that makes it foolish to look upon language as a self-justifying oracle. Professor Read's maxim is refuted by the evidence of common practice. Native speakers do not believe him, for they frequently correct themselves and sometimes each other. Then, too, babies are native speakers and the plentiful mistakes they make are steadily corrected by their parents, by themselves, and by the rest of the community, until all parties decide that the infant (which means "nonspeaker") has at last learned to speak right. This enforcement of a norm has gone on since speech itself began and for all languages everywhere. The only interruption has come recently in Western societies, where it is now thought proper to stop correcting children as early instead of as late as possible.

Lastly, one might ask why in Professor Read's permissiveness only native speakers are granted a right to play fast and loose with the language. Foreigners have imposed their stumblings and their happy turns of phrase on English for fifteen hundred years; they have, as we say, enriched the mother tongue. Why should the grafting and the mangling stop at the borders of nationality? It doesn't sound hospitable, democratic; a free-for-all should be free for *all*.

One further twist: To speak of linguistic life and evolution is to speak in metaphors. But these particular metaphors—alas—can be used equally well to turn the new imperatives upside down. For example, as a living thing, language must be pruned like a tree, must be tamed and castrated like the horse; its nature must be forcibly modified to produce superior hybrids; it must be doctored to cure its diseases and put off its death. Such suggestions horrify the guardians; their notion of life does not include nurture or disease. And far from being detached and limiting themselves to description and classification, they prescribe as well. What they prescribe is that others should not prescribe. They are defending the democracy of linguistic choices. To them, calling some better and some worse is an "elitist pretension" that will fail in the long run. The prophesy is certainly correct if the prescription is faithfully observed.

Anybody who doubts the connection between the new philology and present-day illiteracy, and between the linguist's peculiar prescriptiveness and a socio-political animus has only to turn to the literature that teachers of English have read—and written—for the last half century. As a result of linguistic doctrine, thirty years ago, the National Council of Teachers of English passed a resolution to express "support for the scientific study of the English language," and recommended that teacher training include "instruction in the methods, results, and applications of that study." The primary aim was "to free school teaching from wasteful and harmful practices." The ultimate aim was to teach "the standard English discovered by descriptive research." (Apparently an English teacher's language must first be discovered by research.)

Twenty-three years later, the same Council passed another resolution affirming "The Students' Right to Their Own Language" and giving as the ground of that right another piece of research: "language scholars long ago denied that the myth of a standard American dialect had any validity. . . . The belief leads to false advice for speakers and writers and immoral advice for humans." Strong language. But forget the political intent, good or bad. The point here is the linking of linguistic research with social and moral advice.

Nor is this all. If you look up "Dictionary" in the latest edition of the *Encyclopaedia Britannica*, you will find the author pointing out that "certain words commonly called obscene have [usually] been omitted [from dictionaries], and thus irrational taboos have been strengthened. If the sex words were given in their alphabetical place, ... the false attitudes in society would be cleansed." With one stroke, the linguist disposes of the category "obscene"—words are only *so-called*—and with another, he cleanses society of attitudes he has decided are false. And he regrets in a later paragraph that the Americans have the habit of rushing to the dictionary to find out what is right. He prefers the English, who adopt a less scholarly attitude, as well they may, having a rather stubborn faith that their well-drilled speechways are right and ought to be maintained.

Not all linguists pursue activist purposes, but the atmosphere of permissiveness for rigid ends remains the prevailing ambient for the teaching of English, of foreign languages, and of whatever else is done under the label of "language arts." Individual teachers may have a good or a poor command of the mother tongue, a gift for teaching it or a rank inability to do so, but the creed of linguistics they possess alike, for it is easily grasped and retained.

No one who grew up in the bad old times or who has read the grammars of those days can deny that the rules were too numerous, not very liberal in spirit, and sometimes unjustifiable. It was absurd to make war against splitting an infinitive and ending a sentence with a preposition, and it was misguided to promote genteelism. Yet it is curious to note with what passion millions of English speakers, when they read or write today, still worship these preferences and prohibitions just as they keep rushing to the dictionary. It seems as if there were in most people a deep desire for more rules in the difficult art of saying what one means. People still expect that their offspring will develop adequate ways of self-expression. What can the school do? The struggle toward clear utterance involves mainly vocabulary and grammar—more exact words and words better put together. But help toward these results can hardly be given under the limitations of respect for dialect and misusage and tolerance of wayward syntax.

As for the teachers willing and able to teach good English, they have to contend with another limitation in their training: the old genteelism has been replaced by the prose of the education textbook. That its jargon is fostered in schools was shown in a study done at the University of Chicago by Professor Joseph Williams of the English Department. Teachers in that city gave high grades for written work that sounded formal and stuffy, and low grades to what was put in simple and concrete terms.

What about grammar? The very name these days denotes a predicament. The descriptive grammars since the time of Henry Sweet have been much too extensive and complicated to teach. Every advance in research has added to the number and variety of elements, coupled with new theories of meaning and function. All that these efforts have contributed to the classroom is the destruction of the old terminology, plus another cliché: "English is not Latin." Any grammatical framework resembling the Latin is taboo, which leaves the field open for divergent systems and their tangled terminologies. Phonological, generative, structuralist, transformationist, "grammar of sets," and other labels have been attached to school grammars, all intricate and all taking for granted what I quote from a good specimen: "the central concern of this book is with the system or systems of English Grammar, not with errors that are made or might be made. . . ." And then the refrain: "There is no reason to be horrified by bad sentences. All of us make bad sentences in speaking, and great care and sensitivity must be used in correcting anyone in any circumstances." Fine encouragement for removing illiteracy.

But modern grammars tax more than the moral sense. One "transformational" grammar, several hundred pages thick, is dense reading even for an adult who knows grammar. Here is how it explains to ninth-graders the switch from active to passive voice: "The passive transformation applies only to kernel sentences which contain a transitive verb and its object. In this transformation, the object becomes subject and *be* and the participle morpheme are inserted before the verb. The subject optionally appears at the end after the preposition by." To make it all clear, the text adds: "We can state the rule in this way:

$$NP_1 + Aux + V_T + NP_2$$
$$NP_2 + Aux + be + \text{participle} + V_T + (by + NP_1).\text{"}$$

Such grammars try to be complete, yet they leave out one essential: pedagogy, the art of teaching. It is an omission observable in many other subjects. Up-to-date-ness has tended to blot out the fact that beginners must begin at the beginning with what is simple; subjects must be artificially simplified—if need be, falsified. The refinements, the exceptions to rules, the depths discoverable by advanced analysis must come after a basis has been solidly laid. Anything else is like wanting to carve the ornament before the pillar is built—pre-$posterism$.

But enough of negatives. Polemic is for clearing the ground. If language is not a live creature restlessly evolving, what is it? It is a work of art, a collective work of art, a work of collective art. The English language in particular is a monumental work, which induces awe in anyone who reflects on its past. English goes back, by way of the Indo-Germanic tongues of Europe, to a time beyond the birth of Sanskrit and to the presumed original of all the languages of the West. English has repeatedly strengthened its vocabulary by drawing on these languages in their later forms, as well as on others outside their kin. And it has domesticated these borrowings while smoothing down its own structures and inflexions, making itself the most flexible as well as the richest language on earth. Millions of minds have collaborated in this perfecting—an anonymous, democratic achievement of the first magnitude. No other language comes close to possessing the same merits. As the young William James put this comparison in a vivid image when studying in Dresden: "German is without any of the modern improvements."

The modern improvements have come both by addition and by

subtraction—by changes. But it is far from true that all the changes have come from ignorance or mindlessness. Loving attention, solicitude for needs, intense care about logic and art have been lavished on the English language by speakers and writers who have addressed the public. The work of printers and publishers has given permanence to happy innovation. The linguists are at fault when they dismiss the written word and make a fetish of the spoken. If they consorted more with good books they would find how much of the speech they record originated in written literature, including the law and the sciences—terse idioms, metaphors buried in words, short cuts in syntax, as well as innumerable bright sayings, now clichés and platitudes.

The bearing of this unbroken history is that language belongs as much to the realm of aesthetics as to any other. Scholars may study language as a use of certain organs, as a system of symbols, or as a social institution and draw conclusions about physique, class, nationality, morals, or whatever. But when they study sounds, forms, and meanings they are working in the domain of aesthetic criticism. That is why it is always proper to pass judgment on the current language, reprove its misuse, and defend its subtleties and distinctions. Speakers and writers have a vested interest in the merits of the tongue they work with, exactly as other professionals guard their investments and privileges.

Writers are also capable of doing harm. Modern writers have done as much damage to rhetoric and its teaching as the scientificos. If on one side the famous linguist Leonard Bloomfield said: "Linguists naturally have no respect for words," on the other I can quote the French poet Apollinaire—an adult friend of my childhood days—who was more than half serious when he said to me: "You see, if I want to, I can make *archipelago* mean *blotting paper*." Besides wanting to amuse a schoolboy, he was asserting the power of the poet to join words in untried ways that revigorate them and mark the difference from newspaper prose. This creativeness can go too far. As practiced by poets, novelists, and critics during the past hundred years it has overshot its goal and destroyed the very standard by which original creation can be appreciated, leaving the western languages battered and depleted.

Creative freedom can defeat itself because novelty can be felt only in relation to a perceived norm, just as rhythmic freedom can only be felt against a regular meter. When the norm is obscured by heedless violations, interest gradually disappears. *Archipelago* may evoke *blotting paper* the first time artistry makes the mind jump the gap, but after a myriad imitations, no odd couplings will evoke anything at all.

From poetry in which words and syntax form puzzles to be worked out, sometimes with the help of footnotes, to novels and plays that re-create "reality" by reproducing the fractured utterance of daily life or the fluid confusion of the stream of consciousness, the strain put on language has been intense and unremitting. And latterly, critics and theorists of literature, thick with jargon and top-heavy in syntax, have found fulfillment, like their colleagues in literature proper, by flouting the reader's expectation of tolerable prose. Earlier ages have been as innovative, but in their creations and borrowings they paid heed to the genius of the language and shielded its serviceability. The common instinct was to resist confusion; now many of our respected masters promote it—and are at once copied by the advertisers, the media, and the schools.

For example, whoever wants to see how *Finnegans Wake* reaches the infant mind need only look at a newsletter devoted to the interests of gifted children. It features a contest called *Spallenge*, a term intended to mean "Spin-Off" and "Challenge" at one stroke. The contest invites the creation of new vocables on the same plan; they are called "sqwords," the *sq* to suggest *squeeze*. Twenty-two gifted children have won the privilege of seeing their name and address in the newsletter by contributing such creations as *picalad* (from pickle and salad), *Greethology* (from Greek and mythology), *trivicted*, (from tried and convicted), *treaf* (from tree and leaf), and *authustrated* (from author and illustrated).

The adult inventors of this pastime evidently fail to see that they are teaching, indeed, licensing, corruption—of the language, of exact thought and of its clear expression. Does anyone say "tree leaf" or "author illustrated"? Is there any earthly need for either expression? And supposing there were, would the collapsed syllables convey it? At what cost of guesswork and with what feelings on the part of the puzzled reader or listener? Obviously, no concern for him occurred at any point.

It is of course possible to think without words, but only for a short time. Continuity and recall need the most definite signs available, and these in turn are best fixed by visible marks—writing. Linguistics, though, has decided that the language is the spoken tongue exclusively. How the "science" could last a week without the written word is hard to imagine. In writing, we see our thoughts begin to take the sharp outline that discloses the gaps between them and the flaws within. So true is this that the current failure of the schools to "teach thinking" has been plausibly traced to the advent of multiple-choice testing which has replaced essay writing.

Other "tests" also interfere. The common idea that any forms of speech and writing are good when they achieve "effective communication" is a half truth. Carolino's notorious manual for teaching English to the Portuguese is full of sentences like: "Apply you at the study during that you are young." They are perfectly intelligible, but not English. Right now, ordinary students think they communicate well enough for their needs—and they do. On that score, I had no answer to the student who, seeing his paper full of marginal queries, cried out: "You knew what I meant all the time!" He was right, but had to be told (in softened terms) that I had understood without pleasure or interest, that I had encountered nothing but a dull and sullen mind.

To put the case another way, unless language is regarded as a work of art and treated as we treat efforts to paint and compose music, there is no tenable reason for setting themes and demanding precise diction, correct idiom, economical syntax, varied rhythm, suitable tone, adroit linkage and transitions—in short, no reason for good writing. Some may object that it is hard enough to get plain, decent prose from average students without asking for "art." The rejoinder is that plain and decent, simple and direct are already "art"—and difficult. Since we teach Art in the usual sense—drawing and music—why should we cast the art of language in a separate and unequal role?

On the same principle, the word *language* should be kept to its proper use. Mathematics is not a language; neither is music, nor the Morse code, nor the dance movements of honey bees. The title of R. P. Blackmur's essays *Language as Gesture* is a deplorable concession to the craze for metaphor, suggesting as it does its counterpart, "Gesture as Language." These catchwords repeat the fallacy of equating language with communication, while forgetting that language was developed to *improve* on gesture. Language is language— a unique, *un*comparable creation, and until we readopt this fruitful tautology as our guide to thought and teaching, we shall continue to fail in both. Perhaps all composition classes should begin by reading chapters 18 and 19 in Book II of Rabelais, where the great English scholar, Thaumaste, debates against Panurge entirely by making signs with his arms and hands. He only confesses himself beaten when Panurge thumbs his nose at him and with his fingers distorts his face into a hideous grimace.

In short, the mystique of "communication" is overdone. Among the peoples of the earth most of the trillions of words emitted every minute are not for communication; they are for self-expression. The speaker wants to utter and cares little whether the listener follows, as is shown by the fact that when the speaker stops he stays absorbed in his own train of thought, waiting for an opening to resume speech. That *some* communication takes place in the world is an intermittent miracle brought about less by free desire than by sheer necessity.

The free desire is for self-expression. Language is anchored so deep in our feelings that when they stir we must speak. Likewise, it is mixed feelings that prevent expression. This accounts for the young student's saying that he has nothing to write about, and for what is called writer's block. But when the feelings are both strong and clear, they struggle for language that fits the intent and is aesthetically pleasing. That double goal inspired the makers of language itself. With the material of words as with any other, the work cannot be made right without a strenuous effort, a continual choice and compromise among conflicting demands. The practical test—does it communicate?—is indeed relevant, at the end. The test varies with the occasion and the audience, but intrinsic rightness does not. Rightness is what satisfies the writer for the sake of his own mind. It makes his thought into an object and confirms his sense of power over language. If the student is not taught to feel that need and that pride, he will be content with fumbling words, or possibly miserable because he knows his lack of means for self-expression.

These predicaments and confusions force us back to the question, What to teach in order to dispel them? There is no remedy in sight but the two branches of practical rhetoric, grammar and diction. Let the grammar be artificial as possible, not descriptive of all the vagaries of English; give up all the new terminologies—*head word*, *catenation* and the rest; use the traditional names derived from bad old Latin. These names persist even in the most *moderne* grammars, as we saw above in a quoted passage from one of them; and it is noticeable that people to whom that set of terms is second nature (perhaps because they have had some Latin) can not only write well but also help others analyze their troubles.

The role of grammar is to make conscious the ways in which a language unites meaning and function, which is why grammar is difficult for those who already know the language: function and meaning are fused and seem indivisible. To objectify each role does not require hundreds of pages and thousands of rules. Professor Arn Tibbetts of the University of Illinois has made and successfully taught from a syllabus only a score of pages long.

As to vocabulary, everything about words can be made to arouse curiosity—form, origin, usage, cognates, connotation, logic, and inconsistencies. In fact, until anesthetized by poor teaching, children give a good deal of thought to words; they have had the job of learning to speak a difficult language without books or classes, and they go on looking for clues to the system, finding it wayward, and often venturing analogies of their own. In their school work, the only imperatives should be: no jargon, no fancy metaphors, no pretentiousness masquerading as creativity. And one rule must never be broken: no writing of themes without reading books.

These readings had better not be from the flavorless prose anthologized for college freshmen, nor from the works of contemporaries who "experiment." The standard language is the proper medium for the exercises of teaching, reading, and writing. Standard, despite the council of English teachers, is nothing elitist or tyrannical. It is the product of both art and accident, of both the poet and the people. It is the most ecumenical form of expression, because it permits anyone who makes a little effort to enter into the largest treasury of thought and knowledge, as compared with the narrow, exclusive world of a dialect or trade jargon.

As for the contents of Standard, the only indication is usage. But this must be understood as subject to two conditions often forgotten: Time and Judgment. The new use of a word or use of a new word may be widespread, but it does not become good usage until time passes and overwhelming approval occurs—no one can predict when. "Hand me them pliers" has been said in English for six hundred years and it is not yet Standard; *invite* looks like a perfectly good noun, but writers still keep it out of their prose. To observe these conventions does not make one a purist or a reactionary. For my part, I wish we said *sparrowgrass* instead of *asparagus*, that *I ain't* were good formal English, and that *who* never declined into *whom*. But I am doubtless ahead of my time.

The learner, in respecting usage and the rules like his elders, is not a creature unjustly regimented; he is an apprentice craftsman. He should regard himself as such, that he may soon acquire the confidence enabling him to "vote"—not in the ballot box, but on paper, by choosing one word and rejecting another, by resisting the slovenly, and by accepting happy novelties. His use of Standard for clarity will mark him not as a temperamental conservative, but as a thoughtful conservationist. No one has yet explained why language alone of all human handiwork should not be tended and kept in good repair by the use of intelligence. It would seem a moral duty besides, for language is a rich estate of which we are only the stewards. Its creation by the peoples of the past obligates us to hand it over to the peoples of the future in as good condition as we found it in. That is the true democracy of the matter, as opposed to the condescension of the linguists, who boast of having "no respect for words" and who urge upon the hoi polloi corruption unlimited, while they themselves continue to write in standard prose remarkable chiefly for its would-be scientific vocabulary and its inadequacy when teaching grammar to the young.

Toward the Twenty-First Century

Sooner or later, the sophisticated person who reads or hears that Western civilization is in decline reminds himself that to the living "the times" always seem bad. In most eras voices cry out against the visible decadence; for every generation—and especially for the aging—the world is going to the dogs. In 1493—note the date—a learned German named Schedel compiled and published with comments the *Nüremberg Chronicle*. It announced that the sixth of the seven ages was drawing to a close and it supplied several blank pages at the end of the book to record anything of importance that might yet occur in what was left of history. What was left, hiding around the corner, was the opening up of the New World and a few side effects of that inconsequential event. A glance at history, by showing that life continues and new energies may arise, is bound to inspire skepticism about the recurrent belief in decline.

But sophistication—and skepticism—should go a step further and ask why that same phenomenon recurs; in other words, the historical-minded should look into the meaning and cause of the undying conviction of decline. One cause, one meaning, is surely that in every era some things are in fact dying out and the elderly are good witness to this demise. Manners, styles of art and politics, assumptions about the aim of life or the nature of man and the universe change as inevitably as fashions in dress; and just as no one could deny that men's stiff collars two inches high have vanished into the attic of history, so no one should deny that less tangible entities—say, the idea of "a man of honor"—have vanished too. The very words look quaint and evoke no answering emotion. What is involved here is the vivid faith and the cultural form, not the underlying reality that there are always honest and dishonest men. If such faiths and forms are considered good by a generation that grew up to value them, that generation will experience at their passing a legitimate feeling of loss.

The very notion of change, of which the twentieth century makes such a weapon in the advocacy of every scheme, implies the notion of loss; for in society as in individual life many desirable things are incompatible—to say nothing of the fact that the heedlessness or violence with which change takes place brings about the incidental destruction of other useful attitudes and institutions. Right now for example, one can ask whether all over the world the idea of a university has not been battered without hope of recovery for a long time. This impression, if correct, has nothing to do with the merits of the cause that produced the attack: the historian notes results in the way an insurance assessor notes a broken shopfront.

Before one can assess with the same detachment the extent to which the hitherto dominant Western civilization is damaged or breaking up, one must recall still another historical datum, which is that entire civilizations do perish. The tremendous endings of Greece and Rome are not a myth. True, life somehow continues after the fall, but it is that very "somehow" which tells us that something above mere existence has disappeared. That something is what we call civilization. It is an expression of collective life cast in determinate ways, an expression that includes power, "growth," a joyous or grim self-confidence, and other obvious signs of a going concern. But it consists also of tacit individual faith in certain ideals and ways of life, seconded by a general faith in the rightness of the scheme. It follows that widespread disbelief in those intangibles, and the habits they produce in day-to-day existence, brings on the dissolution of the whole.

The only question then is: How deep goes the disbelief? For history shows both big and little decadences. Decadence means "falling off," and it is possible for a civilization to experience a lesser fall from trust in its own ways without wrecking the entire fabric. The passage from what we call the High Middle Ages to the Renaissance and Reformation was one such falling away and new beginning. The time just before the French Revolution was another. At these moments—roughly the end of the fourteenth century and the end of the eighteenth century—Europe saw old institutions crumble, long-accepted thoughts dissolve, feelings fade away, and new ones take their place.

Those were "epochs," which strictly speaking means *turnings*. The old system comes to what looks like a halt, during which all the familiar things seem empty or wrong. Despair, indifference, the obsession with cruelty and death, the Samson complex of wanting to bring down the whole edifice on one's head and the heads of its retarded upholders—those passions seize the souls of the young generations and turn them into violent agents of change, or disabused skeptics and cynics. From both the activists and the negators come the new ideas and ideals which permit the march of civilization to continue. But it can also happen that not enough new ideas, no vitalizing hopes, emerge, and civilization falls apart in growing disorder, mounting frustration, and brainless destruction.

The judgment as to what took place during a past era is naturally easier to make than the judgment as to what is happening now. But it is again possible to draw guidance from history and take an inventory of significant activities and institutions so as to gauge the degree to which fruitful novelty is keeping pace with obvious destruction. The state in which we find government, religion, morality, social intercourse, language, the arts, and that ultimate basis of civilized life, public hope, permits us to form at least a tentative conclusion about the magnitude of the present *epoch*.

Government is first in the list because first in importance. Many would disagree, but that is in itself a symptom of the contemporary condition. For sixty years or more, advanced opinion in the West has regarded politics and politicians as beneath contempt and the state as an imposition and an imposture. The law and its enforcers are increasingly held in opprobrium as mere tools of "the power group," variously defined but deemed to have won its position largely by fraud and coercion.

Meanwhile crime stalks the capitals of the world, and its suppression is neither feasible nor in keeping with enlightened thought. The value of the state can stand no higher than the utility of its laws, which in turn must command public support and approval. Though the Western system of justice is perhaps the most solicitous ever devised to protect the rights of the accused, its administration has bogged down, and the march of mind has substituted the idea of illness and treatment for that of evil intent and penalty. Doctrines on the subject are moreover confused, with resulting disparities in pleading, sentencing, and paroling which can only wind up as manifest injustice.

Overcrowded and antiquated prisons provoke justifiable riots, and while some prisoners linger awaiting trial, others escape or revolt or come to the end of their sentence after a much abridged term. Nine years is the usual length of the "life" sentence that replaces the "cruelty" of capital punishment. But recidivism is high, robbery with violence is common and enjoys a large immunity, and the criminally insane when released repeat their obsessive horrors— the fit counterpart of what is practiced upon them during their periods of confinement. As in so many realms of social existence, Western man has all the right ideas except that which would turn them into actualities. The net result is contempt for law, for the state that enforces it, and for the governors that still believe in both.

If we ask whether this marks a decadence, we need only observe that the present outlook contrasts sharply with that of a century ago, when the citizen took pride and satisfaction in being an amateur lawyer and parliamentarian. The constitution, the electoral campaign, the jury, and the vote ruled the imaginations of men. The courts and other public authorities earned the respect of the vast majority; they were regarded as the creations of the sovereign people, and such respect and origins helped them to function. Today these same ideas and words call forth only derision. "Law-abiding," "law-and-order" are terms vaguely synonymous with "reactionary." The police are often considered a corrupt, ineffectual part of the body politic, just as that body itself is felt to be a domination by evil forces over simple human nature. These changes mark the end of the liberal ideal, which saw in universal suffrage the key to self-government and in the rule of law the promise of a good society. So far has this ideal sunk that the rightness of any minority has become an axiom, and more and more people feel themselves to be not sovereign, but shamefully oppressed—a desperate minority.

In the place of the former attitude toward the state stands what might be called for short the Marxist analysis. It does not stem from Marxist propaganda alone; but its spirit is that which informs the literature of Marx and his disciples, the spirit of exposure and revelation, the animus of a war against appearances, the search for a reality made up of conspiracies and their victims.

It is a democratic spirit insofar as the passion for equality naturally stimulates envy and suspicion; but it is also a racist spirit in that it attributes virtues and violated rights to one group, wickedness and wrongful supremacy to another. In this sense, visibly, women are a race oppressed by the race of men; the old, the white, and the "bourgeois" are races unjustly dominant over the race of the young, the colored, the poor, and so on down a long list. *La guerre des races* is fought in every public place and public print. The net effect cannot but be lowering, even when nothing discreditable is revealed: the act of digging-to-uncover tells its own accusatory tale and further reduces public faith in what is.

From the point of view, not of what is thus tarnished, but of the art of governing taken in the abstract, it is clear that the incessant eroding of faith and trust must in the end nullify all public authority and with it the general will. When the general will does not habitually prevail over particular wills, nothing is left but the arbitrary acts of improvised centers of power.

The evidence for this conclusion is seen today in the myriad demonstrations occurring all over the world, sometimes against dire oppression, more often against perfectly legal but unpopular measures, and sometimes again from habit, with no defined object in mind, save expressing hostility to whatever is established. The word *Establishment*, torn from its precise meaning, now denotes any institution, even benevolent (such as the fire department), which is tainted with having existed prior to the mood of protest.

Another name for that mood is Civil Disobedience, also a term divorced from its true meaning, which was: defiance of a bad law to show that it was bad, by accepting the consequences of breaking it. Now civil disobedience is the breaking of any law so as to show that existing society commits injustices at large, on which ground the lawbreaker claims immunity. All forms of disruptive protest have this in common that they substitute the pressure of group blackmail for the force of law and put both the law and the officers of government on the defensive as usurpers.

In countries that have traditions and charters of popular sovereignty, these outbreaks are protected by the guaranteed rights of assembly, petition, and strike. But the physical destruction, obscene libel, and interruption of daily life which now mark "petitioning" go far beyond these rights as originally defined. The interpretation of burning the flag as "a statement" guaranteed under free speech is correct only in the context of revolution. The falling away throughout is from the idea of systematic government itself.

In countries where liberalism never won a firm seat—generally those of Eastern Europe, Asia, and Latin America—these extreme ways of political action may seem to be indigenous: coups d'état, civil war, and assassinations serenely continue their long history. They have provided in the past a rough substitute for general elections and a fitful tempering of despotism. But nowadays these uses of force have taken on a new aspect. Formerly, an uprising was an act of war; force was met with force, men died, and no one was astonished. Now uprisings large and small, kidnappings and killings of hostages, and hijackings of planes are expected to be acknowledged as legitimate means of communication between the people and their governors or one people and another. Vandalism and riot having become channels of free opinion, authority must be patient, must withhold force and enter into negotiations, often on the simple terms of "Accept all our demands, or we will do worse."

What Western civilization is witnessing, in short, is the last phase of the great emancipation promoted in the eighteenth century, and that last phase resembles the first, when all enlightened men agreed that authority and the state were always and *a priori* in the wrong. Whenever this feeling holds, any retaliation is necessarily "against the people" and thus a crime. What was then theory is now practice based on the injunction *écrasez l'infâme*. Intellectual opinion leans automatically toward the objector, supports local passion against any central authority, and denounces all sanctions. In other words, power has ceased to be legitimate except when the people take it into their hands. If, as is only fair, we entertain the belief that this conclusion may be justified by enormous, incurable evils on the part of those who rule, then the decadence is from both sides, and the structure of civilization no longer has either the faith or the power to sustain itself.

Under the now universal populism—since even the totalitarian regimes profess to embody it through the "People's Republic," the "People's Democracy," or whatnot—a perpetual referendum or plebiscite would be required to bring into being a new kind of sovereignty. But total consultation is hardly workable in the day-to-day conduct of government, if indeed continuous participation in public affairs is compatible with the other demands of civilized existence. At the present time, in nations not ruled by a dictatorship, the verdict on many issues is more and more often rendered by groups that are or that imitate professional revolutionary cells. To the degree that students all over the world have taken a hand in politics, that is the pattern they have successfully adopted for quick results.

The original model of rule by collective resistance and organized menace has of course been legally at work in the West almost since the start of the period under review: the trade unions, wielding the strike, the closed shop, as well as other devices for regimenting their own members have taught the public the power of direct action by groups. It is gradually replacing rule by individuals supposedly free, who delegate their unit of power to a legitimate authority.

The international scene has of course displayed this kind of behavior for a long while. Bargaining by outrage is an old game. The twentieth century has only added its peculiar tone of vulgar arrogance and boastfulness, aimed at impressing the home front. But the kidnapping and ransoming of envoys, the storming of embassies, and the hatred of foreigners on grounds of "policy" take us back to the primitive times, the Venetian days, of diplomacy. All in all, the growing resemblance between the traditional anarchy of the great powers and the anarchy within each nation marks the decline of the very idea of nationality.

And yet, when a principle happens to be invoked as the reason or occasion for modern outbreaks against the state, the principle generally belongs to the established liberal-socialist agenda: it is "Down with colonialism"—or racism or capitalism. Outbursts of hostility directed at another country spring from these same principles. No new ones, no practical or utopian schemes of society, have emerged in the present century. This lack may have a bearing on the prospects of Western civilization. Besides being unoriginal, the ideals and doctrines now at war are also undisputed in the sense that they continue to exist without support from deep philosophical conviction. Just as all regimes are "for the people," so groups and classes are "for equality and justice" and "against poverty and discrimination." Imperialism (colonialism) has no proponents left; racism as an official policy is restricted to the southern tip of Africa; and capitalism has been so modified that it is at many points indistinguishable from communism, itself also hybridized. Nobody supports the view that the poor are necessary to society or that "inferiors" exist or have a role to play in some hierarchical order. Egalitarianism is affirmed as universally as pauperism is condemned.

Indeed, the only political ism surviving in full strength from the past is nationalism. This was partly to be expected from the liberation of so many colonies simultaneously, beginning in the 1920s. But this nationalism differs from the old in two remarkable ways: it is not patriotic and it does not want to absorb and assimilate. On the contrary, it wants to shrink and secede, to limit its control to its own small group of like-minded we-ourselves-alone. It is in that sense racist, particularist, sectarian, minority-inspired.

In truth, it flourishes as an expression of the antinomian passion which is the deepest drive of the age. In Asia and Africa, the fission of kingdoms and regions into smaller states, and of these states again into smaller ones, shows an impatient mistrust of all central authority, regardless of its source or form. In Europe, nearly every old nation has one or more "subnations" demanding independence—Scotland and Wales from England; Brittany from France; Catalonia and the Basques from Spain. The rage for absolute freedom is virulent. Ireland is in civil war. Little Belgium is rent by strife between two linguistic groups, and her great university has had to be split into two. Canada faces the same threat. Germany is a gerrymander. To the east and south, Balkanization has been overlaid but not extinguished by Soviet domination. Cyprus is a battlefield. In the Far East, unity, never great, is less and less. No sooner is Pakistan free of that imperial monster India than East Pakistan cries out for liberation from the imperial monster West Pakistan, whence Bangladesh.

In short, the one political and social ideal, the one motive power of the time is Separatism, no matter what other rags of older philosophy it masquerades under. If this is not yet Breakdown, it is undeniably Breakup.

Further evidence of disintegration comes from the churches in the form of ecumenism (counterpart of populism), and of "the Underground" (counterpart of revolution). That the Catholic Church, long the model of hierarchical organization, should revise its doctrines with the aid of a large representative assembly is nothing new. What is new is that the rather impolitic decrees subsequent to the Second Vatican Council should be flouted by groups of priests who maintain that they are "not attacking" the authority they defy. The same contention is made by individuals in every church. Ministers take a stand against their governing synods on this or that article of faith, on ritual or private conduct, and call the public to witness whether their autonomy is not in truth justified by the act of challenge itself.

As in the rest of society, the odd new idea is that authority exists to ratify the decisions of its declared enemies. Time has not yet shown whether such an arrangement can continue beyond its first application by the first dissidents. For the time being, responsible authorities hesitate to find heresy, to unfrock or disqualify, not so much afraid as ashamed of wielding any power at all, imbued as they are with the global principle of whatever is is wrong.

A frequent characteristic of dissolving times is—almost by definition—their tendency to blur distinctions of purpose and function. Men and institutions find themselves desiring to fuse aims, activities, and moods formerly held separate. This urge does not contradict the political separatism; it is in keeping with the resolve to *undo*, to remove barriers and recover a primal unity of being with others of one's kind. It is the will to mix, merge, and forget. The business conglomerate is a conspicuous example. It diversifies not alone for commercial safety, but out of a reckless pleasure in flouting industrial specialization: the new corporation produces bathroom fixtures with the right hand and art books with the left. Similarly, the shopping center offers everything—the consecrated chapel for the weary next to the concourse of groceries, the bank, and the dry cleaner—"all under one roof." Students have sought and won the right to eat in libraries and make love in dormitories. The church succeeds in attracting new young worshipers by freshening up the service with their favorite combo; while a rebellious priest thinks he has struck a blow for religion by marrying a couple in a subway station.

The arts have on this point been excellent instructors. What is "mixed media" but the conglomerate in aesthetics, coming after the demonstration that machinery and sculpture, or paint and glued paper, are one? And when actors play in the round or in the nude ("the way we all are born"), or again, when they mingle with the audience as part of their role, what are they saying but that life knows no barriers and distinctions? Sex itself, of which the very name means "cut apart," has logically ceased to be regarded as a demarcation.

In many persons, too, mystical feelings of the same fusing-and-merging kind impel them to beliefs and practices adapted from Buddhism and other creeds, in which the individual strives to lose identity and consciousness of self. This strain of thought has long existed in Western civilization, but it now appears congenial to a far greater variety of people; it has come to seem less eccentric, more in tune with the still more common hostility to the European civilization which, according to such critics, has "ruined" the rest of the world.

Another tradition working to the same end and now very powerful is primitivism—the rage to simplify, return to the innocent beginning of things, and start afresh. This motive inspired the Protestant Reformation; it also drove Gauguin and others to the South seas, to any unspoiled retreat. This longing to start afresh is perpetuated in literary examples—the Crusoe fantasy and the Walden instinct—though strictly speaking, these models are delusive. Crusoe had a shipful of civilized products or he would have perished; Thoreau brought with him an ax, a bag of nails, some beans, and other forms of capital. But feelings are stronger than facts when it is a question of bringing a civilization to its close. The particular urge that demands renewal at any cost has behind it the tremendous force of unreasoning hate against what seems false and confining. "I feel something within me," said the Chieftain from the North, "that compels me to burn Rome."

If distrust and disaffection are so great, if faith in the achievement and the government of Western man is on the wane, what about faith in the grace and the government of God? Reports of high church attendance alternate with reports of widespread religious indifference. These statistics are probably equally correct. They do not change the plain fact that religious fervor is rare and commands little intellectual support. Nietzsche's observation of eighty years ago that "God is dead" was taken up again recently as a liberating idea, but all it records is that the citizens of the modern industrial world do not habitually reckon with Providence or appeal to a deity. They appeal and reckon with machinery, medicine, money, and the forces of the unconscious. These are not gods: the relation of humble intimacy, sacrifice, and mutual love, is lacking.

Thrown back wholly on themselves, men feel their insufficiency. They see more and more clearly that they are not in control of their individual lives or collective destiny, and that many of their practical goals elude their reach. Because of increasing populations, because of the momentum of material things, it appears harder and harder to accomplish any purpose, even one that commands general agreement. To get pollution out of the air, to provide housing or realize the theoretical possibilities of communication and transportation become "problems" whose solutions recede as time flies. It is doubtless from this growing feeling of impotence in the midst of technique that the heirs of twenty-five hundred years of Western culture develop the anger of frustration leading to vandal revolt. Technique and reason, appearing powerless, are called unnatural.

Liberal thinkers down to very recent days had been confident that education would be the civilizing force sustaining a just government in a good society. The experiment of democratic education was tried with enthusiasm and at a huge cost, compared to the outlay of any earlier civilization. The effort still continues, but with growing dismay. For it now seems clear that education too has its limits. Literacy cannot be spread indefinitely; teachers cannot be mass-produced at will like cars; and, worst defeat, the beneficiaries of free schooling resist or scorn the benefit. Accordingly, the latest "solution," offered like a new-found freedom to a once-hopeful world, is "de-schooling society."

When closely examined, the problem turns out to be not an educational one, not something to do with removing ignorance, but the social demand that the school reconcile the pupil to the ways of society, perhaps to life itself. Seeing the poor, the rich, and the middling all contributing their quotas of vandals and dropouts, seeing youth as a new class, commercially important, but in open warfare with the world, the liberal imagination of educators and social philosophers concludes that here is one more witness to the bankruptcy of "bourgeois values." Like representative government, like capitalism, like traditional religion, the culture that the West has been painstakingly fashioning since Columbus has ceased to serve and satisfy.

This verdict which condemns the middle class as responsible for the evils of the age is not being uttered today for the first time. Nor was it first pronounced by the Marxians or their predecessors and successors in socialism. It is not a purely economic indictment in any case. When the anti-bourgeois commonplaces, now nearly two hundred years old, are repeated today, they imply something other than a call to rescue the proletariat from the oppression of the powerful. They imply guilt for failing to create a better world, the great, rational society. After all, the conception of the general welfare springs from liberal thought itself as it turned away from laissez faire in the nineties and followed the lead of Bismarck and the socialists toward a state affording complete social security. And liberal-socialist thought is a bourgeois invention. Similarly, the "rights of the people" are not in opposition to the "materialism" imputed to the bourgeois as a sin, for surely these "rights" include the people's material prosperity.

Topping these paradoxes is the supreme one that the present spiritual distress and revolutionary surge come at a time of general affluence and high productivity; a time, moreover, when thanks to industry Western civilization has reversed the age-old proportions of rich and poor. It is certainly our shame that fifteen to twenty percent of our most advanced populations are in want, yet it is not by accident that the ratio is no longer what it always used to be— twenty percent in comfort and eighty percent in want. But nothing is harder to bear than the contrast between what is and what might be. The power to create wealth has given mankind a glimpse of universal plenty, and when we find ourselves far from abundance on a global scale, impatience turns into fury.

If we look deeper still than these causes of anguish and disaffection, we find that even a much nearer approach to planetary prosperity would not in fact relieve our pain. Just as when John Stuart Mill, then a young liberal reformer, fell into a deep depression and asked himself whether the instant realization of all his hopes would make him happy, and he answered no, so today the full realization of the Western world's practical concerns would not reconcile and make happy its chief denouncers. It might make the poor and disfranchised happier, but one may wonder for how long, since those already free from want, tyranny, ignorance, and superstition declare themselves the most oppressed and miserable of men and willingly risk what they have in order to smash the system.

This abolitionist outlook is not new either, and it is not radical in the political sense. It is moral and aesthetic, and it was first given form by the artists who came to maturity during or shortly after the French Revolution. It was then that art took over the role that religion had formerly played in holding up to the impure world the divine promise and reproach of a pure one. With the Romanticists, the city of God became the vision of art. It was then also that the bourgeois citizen became an object of hatred and contempt, because he believed in the world—in trade, in politics, in regular hours, a steady life, a safe marriage, sound investments, and a paunchy old age. His moral complacency and artistic philistinism made him appear the enemy of all generous emotion, the antithesis of everything spiritual and selfless in man.

The great popular disillusionment after the failure of revolution in 1848 intensified this antagonism. With the onset of industrialization, the uglification of cities, the visible degradation of the masses, the demagogy and sensationalism of the penny press, the cheapening of taste through the early crude mass production, the raucousness of advertising, the emotional disturbances connected with the change from manual to mechanical work that makes man a cipher—with all these and a dozen other consequences of man's entry into the industrial age, the moral and aesthetic conscience of the West, manifesting itself through its artists, began to repudiate society as a whole. This many-sided denunciation is what Goethe and Hugo, Ruskin and Baudelaire, Shaw and William Morris made plain in verse and prose—and not only they, but hundreds of others in every language of Europe. The despair was universal and the evils depicted remarkably uniform.

Then, after 1870 in Europe, two movements prepared the modern embattled, alienated stance of the arts. One movement took the path of withdrawal, self-enclosure in the "genuine" world of spirit and sensation. Its present-day continuation may be seen in all the groups that use every means to drop out of society and the self, including the industrial, chemical means called drugs. The results are extreme, but the tradition is, as it were, respectable. Bohemia was the first form of counterculture and it is more than a hundred years since Baudelaire justified the "artificial paradise" of drug taking as a necessary antidote to urban life.

The other movement was from the start activist and used art to shock the bourgeois into a realization of his own turpitude. The line from the Naturalists and satirists of the eighties (Zola, Jarry) through the Futurists, Surrealists, Dadaists, and Expressionists to the Existentialists and others of our contemporaries is clear. Indeed, the explosive devices have changed surprisingly little. The dose of shock has merely been increased to keep up with the inflation of all effects. When Genêt became, by Sartre's say-so, an artistic and civic model on the strength of being a gifted thief and homosexual, or when novelists and playwrights have depicted torture, madness, rape, and coprophilia in parables meant to turn upon the public the light of self-reformation, the entire bourgeois class could not but be convinced of its own abominableness. All the while, the less violent writers and dramatists preached from the same book. Joyce and Gide and Proust and D. H. Lawrence and E. M. Forster "show up" the bourgeois and "his" society, dig down into the murk of motive, and prove that not a word can be said for things as they are.

The arts of storytelling being almost wholly devoted to this propaganda, it was left to music and the plastic arts to satisfy the inarticulate emotions of a hard-driven society. Since the first decade of this century the appeal of line, color, and sound has outstripped that of words. But even if many of the compositions in concrete or pigment or tone have furnished the aesthetic pleasure that strengthens the soul, many more have had the effect—intended or not—of once again "facing" the beholder with the despair and disharmonies of his own life. The cult of originality, the need of artists to singularize themselves within the growing mass of the talented, has encouraged the strong and arrogant to administer increasingly brutal shock treatments to the public. This has meant more than merely abandoning representation or simple one-step abstraction from objects. First the work was reduced to mere sensation; then the beholder was excluded by saying that painting is only an act of the painter's, preferably a random act; finally the artist eliminated himself, either by relying on randomness or by preferring to collect and exhibit oddments from the junkheap of industrial society. Dehumanization condemns present man as vile and concentrates the gaze on raw materials—noise, color, line, words as words, in rebuke to the very idea of civilization.

Hence the label "anti" has found ubiquitous uses—anti-hero, anti-novel, anti-art. "Deconstruction" sings the same tune, and the bland acceptance of such labels as descriptive of what is true, right, and progressive is a symbol if not a sign of a general complicity in the work of demolition. Considering this deep self-hatred and the unforgiving thoroughness behind the moves toward complete emancipation from the past, the student of contemporary culture hazards a guess that the current relaxing of morals and manners is rather a consequence than a cause of the general disarray.

In such a state of affairs, decadence—falling away, dissolution— is possible and, indeed, likely. The artists, intellectuals, and publicists of the century have done their work so well that most bourgeois themselves, for all their advanced years and their innate philistinism, feel strong stirrings of sympathy with those who want to devour them and with the classes that want to replace them. In great revolutions the victims (or a large group of them) can be counted on to help. Today one finds throughout Western civilization men in high places who freely confide their disgust and openly envy their antagonists and sometimes subsidize them in secret.

But the inchoate movement for renovation is not so simple as even this double twist would suggest. Among the young there are, as always, manipulators of others' ideals; they have set plans and sure techniques, but their goal is indistinct. Among the idealists (and sometimes within the rebel himself) there is a split in the method of making all things new. The cry of Participation heard in Europe and America points to this uncertainty. Participation means sharing the power, but this in turn means entering the Establishment, joining the bourgeois and working with them. Is this practicable, even if acceptable? The eager invaders are no more sure of the answer than are the factory workers who also want Participation in management: independence and responsibility tug opposite ways. The only settled point is that the new man, the New Left, the New Age, the new wave, the new cry in art, films, dress, lingo, or morals toil together to hasten the work of time and oblivion.

If it were not for the striking convergence of these forces, there would be no point in discussing the character of the turning point which some say we have reached or passed or sighted ahead; and the books by Spengler, Toynbee, Riencourt, Pickman, and others would not furnish catchwords and arguments for general conversation. The civilized frame of mind is always self-conscious, but perhaps none before ours has attained such an extreme of self-consciousness. We owe this sensitivity to our long historical memory, even if buried; to the breadth of our information, which gives us no respite to enjoy the present, for it continually turns into something else; to the peculiarity of our literature and our psychology, alike introspective and ruthless in imputing bad motives, suspicious of the least self-satisfaction; to the bleakness of our science, which shows a purposeless universe of not even harmonious design; and finally to the fears that our great cleverness has raised up—fear of atomic destruction, fear of overpopulation, fear of our massed enemies and, in daily life, fear of all the diseases, mishaps, and dangers that technology creates and incessantly warns about.

All these hurts to sensibility form one cause of the decay of public hope. It may be hazarded as an historical generality that the periods of creation, like the success of particular movements, occur when hope—the vision of Possibility—is vivid in many minds, when it is obvious to all that Construction is possible. Then the presence of obstacles and opposition is only another incentive to struggle. The uphill fight is going to be rewarded by an incomparable view from the summit. This was the feeling among the gifted at the height of the eighteenth century, and again in the great flowering of Romanticism and Liberalism. It sprang up once more after the *fin de siècle* lassitude as our own century began. The Cubist decade was a great producer of models. Then came the catastrophe of the Four Years' War of 1914–1918, which not only swept from the earth innumerable young geniuses, but showed the Western world that it could not protect civilization from its own stupid or evil impulse.

The spirit of the West has never really recovered from that shattering. Lately, scholarship has come to see that for half a century we have been living on the ideas generated during the two decades before that war, 1895 to 1914. In science, art, technology, philosophy, social and political thought, all the new principles were set forth, from aviation, wireless, and motion pictures to abstract art, city planning, aesthetic simultaneity, quantum physics and genetics, relativity and psychoanalysis. We have only elaborated those teachings, or tried, when we could, to evade them by jumping back to earlier models, quite in vain. The question now is whether the events we are witnessing are preparing another open and level ground for a reawakened animal faith and the creation of undreamed-of new things, or whether on the contrary our sullen doings have reached repetition in futility.

While "awaiting confirmation or adversity," as the poet put it, we can recapitulate and take stock each for ourselves. There is no doubt that regarding the outer shell or container of civilization, which is the state, all our efforts tend against aggregation and toward disintegration. Yearning and action alike are moving us toward the small, self-contained unit that can be "free." It may be a wise unconscious preparation for the time when atomic war has pulverized large-scale existence and the survivors must be content with the isolated "villa" (= settlement) of late Roman times. In that case the deliberately minimal modes of living that many cultivate are a sign of remarkable prescience.

But it is also possible that the urge to flee the octopus organization and the distant rule by unseen hands, so as to huddle with a few friends and bemoan our lot or demonstrate against it, will suffer a check. Anarchy goes so far; then it generates repression. Such a reversal would bring on a puritanism of the most relentless kind. Artists, free thinkers, and free lovers who currently denounce the Western countries as police states would from their labor camps long for the good old days. In either event, the present failure of authority is a prime symptom. It tells us that on the all-important question of how to live together, the contemporary world has not a single new idea to offer, not one.

The next diagnostic point is the question of morals and religion. Morality, like religion, has the double aspect of satisfying an emotional need and serving a social purpose. Without morality—some inner restraint—society must assign two policemen to watch every citizen day and night. And without a religion which organizes the facts of life and the cosmos, men seek in vain for the meaning of their existence. Not all can find in art or science a substitute justification; and pure, unreflecting ambition or calculated hedonism is rare and demands special gifts. Great populations without a goal outside themselves will turn to national war or race hatred to find the glow of common sacrifice and the call to transcendence that the human spirit requires. On these points too, at the present time, the Western mind is mute. Popular revivalist religion captures only a few more souls than does subtle philosophic or aesthetic religiosity, leaving a void for the seven devils of partisan hatred to disport in. As for the embodiment of the fundamental decencies through manners, we have not even begun to think about what would be desirable for an overcrowded world. We have only drifted into the casual style, of which the extremes inspire disgust with one's fellow man.

On second thoughts, art and science seem to offer better grounds for complacency. In our time, both have gained enormously in prestige and support; their practitioners are the only admired leaders. Ostensibly, then, art and science are flourishing, which argues a "healthy society." The metaphor of health is misleading—a healthy malignancy kills the patient. The arts are not malignant, but they are either hostile or ambiguous. They mean to awaken the complacent and they succeed. But how long must the lesson last? And what does perpetually teaching it do to the artist himself? The imagination of disaster is a great gift, but after the disaster what? Cassandra's employment ends with her success. One happy thought about the contemporary arts is that they are performing the great task of detaching us from all old models of feeling, seeing, and thinking, in preparation for the indescribable new.

Science too has little to say *comprehensively*. It is none too well integrated within itself. The proliferating specialties, each with its private language and its stream of discoveries, do not cohere and settle large subjects; it has become a matter of pride that science is never done. If that is so, science is not what its founders expected and promised: a solid edifice of knowledge soon to be completed. Rather it is for a few an absorbing activity whose results can never give its patron civilization a cosmos fit for contemplation.

There is not even, for the educated, the prop of an all-embracing speculative philosophy. Ethics and metaphysics are no longer subjects for self-respecting philosophers to think about. For half a century or more, professional thinkers have preferred to analyze language, to attempt the quantification of the intuitive, or to work out the rationale of science. The next-door neighbors of philosophy—psychology and theology—leave the intelligent layman equally uncared for amid a plethora of myths and metaphors, of "personal statements" and social-scientific studies: there is no reconciliation between Ouspensky and Dr. Kinsey. As for the common man, he has been left more than ever at the mercy of his penchant for superstition. Machines domesticated and poeticized by advertising supply the miraculous, while astrology enlivens the newspapers and unidentified flying objects people the heavens.

To be sure, science is now wedded to technology and faithful in its service. Those who do the work retain their enthusiasm for the future, because technology can create abundance and replenish or eke out the supply of natural goods. But there are perplexities; the greatest, how to distribute the product. The Common Market is the furthest the West has gone in mellowing international trade. Internally, the nations are stumped by the politics of economics, and economics by the ways of man. None of this proceeds from ill-will or indifference, except insofar as these vices afflict some of the individuals assigned to execute the endless plans and programs for the rescue of an unhappy world.

So as the last decade of the century opens we find both the social and the intellectual impulses tending toward flight or destruction. The observer feels himself carried back to Saint Augustine's time of fear and anger, to its clamoring band of prophets and thaumaturgists and their beguiled followers or skeptical satirists. If these are not the signs of an emphatic ending, they look uncommonly like it.

Remains one question: if the description is correct, if it is an ending, a thoroughfare leading into the desert, of what magnitude is the predictable pause and turn? To ask this is to push the observer beyond his limits. He can safely say that we are seeing something of greater moment than the close of neoclassicism at the end of the eighteenth century. What is dying out is the individualism and high art of the Renaissance, the fervor of the Reformation, the hopes of liberalism, the zest of the free and patriotic nation-state. But is it more than the close of a brilliant half-millennium? Is it akin to the fall of Rome, the death of paganism, and the turmoil of barbarian clusters under a primitive and precarious Christianity?

Or is it some third phenomenon—for where are now the vigorous, untroubled barbarians and the heroic bishops and missionaries bearing the Word? The many movements that call themselves new are *not* new, except in membership. They still hack away at the old structures. What is wanted is an open conspiracy of genuine Young Turks who will turn their backs on analysis and criticism and re-invent—say—the idea of the university, and show what it can do; who, seeing that bureaucracy is inevitable, will rethink the art of administration and make it work. And when the energies of re-construction revivify the landscape, the fine arts will spontaneously mirror the change, show a new face, and the public, enheartened, will rejoice in the new life.

But—a last consolation for us—as long as man exists, civiliza-tion and all its works also exist in germ. Civilization is not identical with *our* civilization, and the rebuilding of states and cultures, now or at any time, is integral to our nature and more becoming than longing and lamentations.

Bibliographical Note

Several of the chapters in this book have appeared in somewhat different form: "Culture High and Dry" as "Scholarship versus Culture" in *The Atlantic* (November 1984); "The Insoluble Problem: Supporting Art" as "The Insoluble Problem: The Patronage of Art" in *Proceedings of the American Philosophical Society* 131, no. 2 (1987); "Look It Up! Check It Out!" in *The American Scholar* (Autumn 1986); "Where Is History Now?" in *Proceedings of the Massachusetts Historical Society* 95 (1983); "What Critics Are Good For" as "What Are Critics Good For?" as the Annual Humanities Lecture, 92nd Street Y, New York NY, January 25, 1988; "Reckoning with Time and Place" as "The Critic, the Public, and the Sense of the Past" in *Salmagundi* (Fall 1985–Winter 1986); "*Exeunt* the Humanities" as "This Business of the Humanities" in *Three Talks by Jacques Barzun*, Northern Kentucky University, 1980; "A Surfeit of Fine Art" as "A Surfeit of Art" in *Harper's Magazine* (July 1986); "The Fallacy of the Single Cause" as "Walter Prescott Webb and the Fate of History" in *Essays on Walter Prescott Webb and the Teaching of History*, eds., Dennis Reinhartz and Stephen E. Maizlish (College Station TX: Texas A & M University Press, 1985), used by permission of the Walter Prescott Webb Memorial Lectures Committee, University of Texas at Arlington; "License to Corrupt" as "Rhetoric and Rightness: Some Fallacies in a Science of Language" in *The Creating Word: Papers from an International Conference on the Learning and Teaching of English in the 1980s*, ed., Patricia Demers (London: Macmillan, and Alberta: The University of Alberta Press, 1986); "Toward the Twenty-First Century" as "The State of Culture Today" in *The Columbia History of the World*, vol. III, eds., Peter Gay and John A. Garraty (New York: Harper & Row, 1972), copyright © 1972 by Harper & Row.

About the Author

Jacques Barzun—scholar, teacher, editor, critic—is an authority on a wide range of subjects, from literature, music, and art, to the superstition of race and the delights of detection. He came to the United States from France in 1920 at thirteen, was graduated from Columbia College in 1927, and taught at Columbia from 1927 to 1975, having been, among other things, Seth Low Professor of History and Dean of Faculties and Provost. He is also a fellow of the Royal Society of Arts and was twice president of the American Academy of Arts and Letters.

Among his best-known works are *Darwin, Marx, Wagner*; *Berlioz and the Romantic Century*; *Teacher in America*; *The House of Intellect*; *A Word or Two Before You Go....*; and *The Modern Researcher* (with Henry F. Graff). His home is in New York City.

About the Editor

Arthur Krystal is a critic and editor who lives in New York. His work has appeared in *The New York Times Book Review, The American Scholar, The Wall Street Journal, The Washington Post Book World,* and *The New Criterion.*